An Experiment With An Air Pump

1799. On the eve of a new century, a house buzzes with scientific experiments, furtive romance and farcical amateur dramatics.

1999. In a world of scientific chaos, cloning and genetic engineering, the cellar of the same house reveals a dark secret buried for 200 years.

Shelagh Stephenson was born in Northumberland and read drama at Manchester University. She has written five original plays for BBC Radio. These include *Darling Peidi*, about the Thompson and Bywater murder case, which was broadcast in the Monday Play series in 1993; a Saturday Night Theatre, *The Anatomical Venus*, broadcast in the following year; and *Five Kinds of Silence* (1996), which won the Writers' Guild Award for Best Original Radio Play and the Sony Award for Best Original Drama. Her first stage play, *The Memory of Water*, opened at the Hampstead Theatre, London, in July 1996, and her second, *An Experiment With An Air Pump*, joint winner of the 1997 Peggy Ramsay Award, opened at the Royal Exchange Theatre, Manchester, in February 1998. She is currently working on new commissions for the Hampstead Theatre and the Royal National Theatre.

by the same author

The Memory of Water & Five Kinds of Silence

An Experiment With An Air Pump

Shelagh Stephenson

Methuen Drama

Methuen Drama

Copyright © 1998 by Shelagh Stephenson
The right of Shelagh Stephenson to be identified as the author of this
work has been asserted by her in accordance with the Copyright,
Designs and Patents Act, 1988

First published in Great Britain in 1998
by Methuen Publishing Limited

Methuen Drama
A&C Black Publishers Ltd
36 Soho Square
London W1D 3QY
www.methuendrama.com

5 7 9 10 8 6 4

A CIP catalogue record for this book
is available from the British Library

Papers used by Methuen Drama are natural, recyclable products
made from wood grown in sustainable forests. The manufacturing processes
conform to the environmental regulations of the country of origin.

ISBN 0 413 73310 6

Typeset by Deltatype Ltd, Birkenhead, Merseyside

Caution

An Experiment With An Air Pump

for Eoin

An Experiment With An Air Pump was first performed at the Royal Exchange Theatre, Manchester, on 12 February 1998. The cast was as follows:

Fenwick/Tom	David Horovitch
Susannah/Ellen	Dearbhla Molloy
Harriet/Kate	Louise Yates
Maria	Sarah Howe
Roget	Tom Smith
Armstrong/Phil	Tom Mannion
Isobel	Pauline Lockhart

Directed by Matthew Lloyd
Designed by Julian McGowan
Lighting by Peter Mumford

Characters

1799

Joseph Fenwick, *physician, scientist, radical, fifty-five.*
Susannah Fenwick, *his wife, forty.*
Harriet,⎫ *their twin daughters, twenty.*
Maria, ⎭
Peter Mark Roget, *physician, scientist, later of Thesauraus fame, twenty-one.*
Thomas Armstrong, *scientist, physician, twenties.*
Isobel Bridie, *a Scots servant with a twisted spine, twenty-five.*

1999

Ellen, *a scientist, forty. Doubles with Susannah.*
Tom, *an English lecturer, fifty-five. Doubles with Fenwick.*
Phil, *a Geordie builder, twenties. Doubles with Armstrong.*
Kate, *a scientist, friend of Ellen, twenty-five-ish. Doubles with Harriet.*

Act One

Prologue

*Chiaroscuro lighting up on slow revolve tableau involving the whole cast (except **Susannah/Ellen**), which suggests Joseph Wright's painting,* An Experiment on a Bird in the Air Pump. **Fenwick** *takes the role of the scientific demonstrator. Revolve continues slowly throughout this scene. The bird flutters in the glass dome. Strategically placed above the audience are four large projections of Wright's painting.* **Ellen**, *dressed casually in loose trousers, T-shirt, deck shoes, is looking up at them. Two dressers come on with her costume, wig, shoes etc., for the part of* **Susannah**.

Ellen I've loved this painting since I was thirteen years old. I've loved it because it has a scientist at the heart of it, a scientist where you usually find God. Here, centre stage, is not a saint or an archangel, but a man. Look at his face, bathed in celestial light, here is a man beatified by his search for truth. As a child enraptured by the possibilities of science, this painting set my heart racing, it made the blood tingle in my veins: I wanted to be this scientist; I wanted to be up there in the thick of it, all eyes drawn to me, frontiers tumbling before my merciless deconstruction. I was thirteen. Other girls wanted to marry Marc Bolan. I had smaller ambitions. I wanted to be God.

The dressers hook her into a tight corset over her T-shirt.

This painting described the world to me. The two small girls on the right are terrified he's going to kill their pet dove. The young scientist on the left is captivated, fascinated, his watch primed, he doesn't care whether the dove dies or not. For him what matters is the process of experiment and the intoxication of discovery. The two young lovers next to him don't give a damn about any of it.

The dressers help her into her dress and shoes, put on her wig.

But the elderly man in the chair is worried about what it all means. He's worried about the ethics of dabbling with life and death. I think he's wondering where it's all going to end. He's the dead hand of caution. He bears the weight of all the old certainties and he knows they're slipping away from him, and from his kind. But when I was thirteen, what held me more than anything, was the drama at the centre of it all, the clouds scudding across a stage-set moon, the candle-light dipping and flickering. Who would not want to be caught up in this world? Who could resist the power of light over darkness?

The dressers hand her a fan and leave. The lights change, the projections fade, and as **Susannah***, she joins the tableau.*

Maria   Will he die, Papa?

Fenwick   We'll see, won't we?

Maria   I don't want him to die.

Armstrong   It's only a bird.

Harriet   It's Maria's pet.

Armstrong   The world is bursting with birds, she can get another –

Maria *bursts into tears.*

Maria   I don't want another one. I want this one! I named him for my fiancé.

Harriet   They do have a similar intellectual capacity.

Susannah   Don't start, Harriet.

Roget   Perhaps we could use a different bird . . .

Armstrong   D'you happen to have one on you?

Roget   Well, I could – I'm sure we could find one –

Susannah   Mr Roget, there's really no need to go trampling round the garden with a net, I'm afraid Maria is being a dreadful baby.

Maria   I don't want Edward to die, Papa –

Susannah   Maria, show a little faith, your father would never conduct an experiment unless he was quite sure of the outcome, isn't that so?

Fenwick   You haven't quite grasped the subtlety of the word 'experiment', Susannah –

Maria   He's going to kill Edward!

Armstrong   This goes to prove the point I made earlier, sir: Keep infants away from the fireplace and women away from science.

Fenwick *gives him a long look.*

Fenwick   How old are you now, Armstrong?

Armstrong   I'm about to be twenty-six, sir.

Fenwick   You're an awful prig, has anyone ever told you that?

He performs the experiment. Gasps. The bird flutters out, unharmed.
Maria *gives a cry of delight, general clapping, laughter. Blackout.*

Scene One

Sounds of rioting going on outside – breaking glass, a baying mob, crashes, screams etc.

A chandelier descends from the ceiling and throws out scattered, shimmering light.

A bewildering variety of stuffed birds, animals and reptiles are suspended on strings, mounted on plinths, displayed in cases. A large cluttered desk, piled up with books, a microscope, a skull, bits of bodies and organs pickled in jars, nearby a telescope. Various bits of machinery.

Fenwick *sits at his desk, writing calmly, ignoring the tumult outside.* **Susannah** *sits at a small card table endlessly playing patience, drinking brandy, and growing steadily more intoxicated.*

Roget *hovers anxiously, wincing at some of the more alarming crashes. Occasionally he peers through the telescope.* **Armstrong** *is agitated, glancing at his pocket watch.*

Armstrong   D'you think we're trapped?

Roget *looks through the telescope*

Roget   I can't see a thing. Apart from smoke.

Fenwick (*not looking up*)   Stop fretting for God's sake.

Susannah   That's right, Mr Armstrong. Stop fretting. It's merely a crazed mob, mad on drink and wild for blood. Nothing to fret about.

Fenwick   Any more proposals for the New Year lectures?

Susannah   We could all be burnt in our beds. Probably will be. Hey ho. (*Turns over a card.*) Excellent. Three of spades.

Armstrong (*very agitated*)   I have an appointment.

Fenwick   I'd advise you to forget it. What about these proposals, Roget?

Roget *rummages around in his pockets and produces some sheets of paper. He looks through them.*

Roget   A marked preoccupation with all things dental.

A roar from the crowd outside. He winces at the sound of a huge crash.

Armstrong   Someone ought to put a stop to this.

Roget   Go on then.

Fenwick   Stop agitating and sit down, Armstrong, you're not going anywhere at present –

Armstrong   I was expected ten minutes ago!

Fenwick *turns round to look at him.*

Fenwick   What's the nature of this pressing appointment?

Armstrong *is hesitant. He glances at* **Susannah**.

Armstrong   Dr Farleigh is giving . . . a demonstration.

Pause. **Fenwick** *gives him a long look.*

Fenwick   I see. Well, I'm sure there'll be others.

Armstrong   This is a particularly interesting one.

Susannah   A particularly interesting what?

Armstrong   It's an unusual – it's a very um, singular . . . case, anatomically speaking . . . woman of thirty years, enormously malformed skull –

Fenwick (*briskly*)   Well, it can't be helped. Unless you want to risk your neck out there. Roget, where were we?

Roget   Mr Matthews is offering 'Notes on the Development of Wisdom teeth' and Mr Devenish offers 'On the Early Failure of Pairs of Grinding Molars'.

Armstrong *is still in a state of agitation, pacing up and down, glancing at his watch, and then through the telescope.*

Fenwick   God save us. What else? Oh, sit down, Armstrong, for God's sake. You've missed your appointment and that's the end of it. There's no need to make us all suffer for it.

Armstrong *sits down, furiously.*

Armstrong   This is a bitter disappointment.

Susannah   All life's a bitter disappointment, Mr Armstrong. Take it from me.

Roget   Moving on from teeth, Mr Percy Fellowes would like to offer a learned paper on 'Left Leggedness'. He points out that 'The rule in nature seems to be to bear to the right, and this phenomenon would seem to be universal.'

Fenwick   When Kant said we were living in an age of enlightenment he reckoned without the existence of Percy Fellowes.

Susannah   A very dreary man. Last year he delivered a

lecture on pimples, Mr Roget. Unsavoury and quite unnecessary.

Roget   The piece comprises twenty-three pages and comes complete with illustrations 'which may be passed amongst the audience'.

Susannah   Fortunately his last offering came without supporting diagrams.

Fenwick   Tell him to go hang himself. Perhaps he could produce a learned paper on the universal rules of that particular phenomenon. Give us all some peace.

Roget (*checking off his list*)   Then I take it that's a no to the teeth, and a no to the legs –

Susannah   – I do hope so –

Roget   – moving on, in that case, to the next sub-section, what about Reverend Jessop's offer? 'On the Fundamental Laws of Vegetable Bodies, Whether Plants Have A Principle Of Self Preservation, And The Irritability Of Plants In General.'

Fenwick *turns round.*

Fenwick   We're talking about New Year's Eve for God's sake. The last night of the century. Has this fact bypassed these people? We want something worthy of the past and fired by visions of the future. We want to excite the audience, exhilarate them, we want to celebrate the intellect, march towards a New Jerusalem with all our banners flying. We discussed all this at the last meeting. What did we say our aim was? 'A lively ferment of minds producing a radical vision for the new century.' And what do we get? A botany lesson.

Armstrong   I think botany does come within the brief of Literary and Philosophical, Dr Fenwick –

Fenwick   Bugger it. Bugger botany –

Susannah   He's quite foul-mouthed when he's riled, have you noticed, Mr Armstrong –

Roget   To be fair, sir, I think you'll find the paper neither dull nor irrelevant, in fact it seems to me quite stimulating –

Fenwick   – bugger constipated, dull-as-ditch-water musings –

Susannah   – it's almost a nervous twitch –

Fenwick   – from a bunch of retired curates. They should all be shot.

Roget   – I'll put that down as a possible then –

Fenwick   Have you ever met the Reverend Jessop? A milky, self-righteous, insipid little mannikin with a handshake like a dead fish. The man has piss where his blood should be –

Susannah   Now there I must agree with you.

Fenwick   If he's to lead us into the new century we're all doomed.

Armstrong   With respect, I think you confuse a personal antipathy towards Reverend Jessop with the quality of his proposed lecture.

Fenwick   He can deliver it later in the year. Preferably when I am otherwise engaged. Next.

Armstrong   With respect, sir –

Fenwick   Stop saying that, will you? If there's one phrase that sets my teeth on edge –

Armstrong   – forgive me, but the personal shortcomings of this particular clergyman have no bearing on the rigor or otherwise of his science –

Fenwick   Rubbish, one look at the man is enough to tell you he's a complete fool. He sets out with a premise and trims the world to fit it. What he practices is not science, but a branch of theology.

Armstrong   Objectivity is paramount in these things, you said so yourself, sir. One set of prejudices is as dangerous as another, I think that's how you put it.

Roget   And besides, you've not read the paper. I think you'll find there's not a mention of God in it anywhere –

Fenwick   Very well, very well, you've proved your point. I concede defeat. Passionate aversion has indeed muddied my strict impartiality. I admit it, I make no excuses for it. And I still won't give the man house room. Next.

Armstrong   It's a lost cause, Roget.

Roget   On a lighter note there's Mr Charlton's paper on 'Suffocation and Resuscitation from Apparent Death'. Very popular with the ladies according to the author.

Susannah   Then that's the man for me. Hire him immediately.

Roget   Or Mr Cowgill's on 'The Cunning Ways In Which Animals Conceal Themselves From Their Enemies'?

Fenwick   For God's sake, we want to storm into the next century not doze through it –

Roget   (*scanning his list*)   'The French Revolution. Success Or Failure? Its Lessons For The New Century.' Dr Cavendish. Or Dr Farleigh: 'Is Progress an Illusion and The Past a Myth?' Now that sounds tremendously interesting –

Fenwick   Better. Depressing, and hardly a celebration, but better.

Roget   A good point for debate though, surely you must admit –

Susannah   Speaking personally, I'd rather have Reverend Jessop and his legs.

Fenwick   What else?

Roget   But, sir, I do think the notion of a mythological past –

Fenwick   Yes yes yes, Roget, stop whimpering, we'll come back to it later. What else?

Roget   'A History of the Flute from Roman Times to the Present Day', I don't think so . . . 'Whelks and their Habitat' . . . I think that fails on the visionary count . . . 'A History Of Northumberland in Watercolours', no . . . 'The Colour Green and Why it is So Generally Diffused in the Plant Kingdom' –

Fenwick   Reverend Jessop?

Roget   I'm afraid so. That seems to be it.

Fenwick   What a collection of dismal drips –

There is an enormous explosion. **Susannah** *stops playing cards.*

Susannah   This is past a joke.

Fenwick   I love a good explosion, don't you? The best tonic in the world is the sound of institutions tumbling. If I could bottle it I'd take a draught every day and live to a hundred. Though, sadly, this is merely a lot of noise signalling nothing whatsoever. Tomorrow morning the only thing to have changed will be the price of fish. If they're lucky.

He turns back to his desk with a sigh.

Armstrong, when you see Farleigh, ask him to call in. There might be something in his gloomy little sermon. And try and find a few more radical offers, can you, Roget? I don't think we could stomach an entire evening listening to that other rot.

He concentrates once again on his work.

Roget   I was wondering, sir, if I might –

Susannah   (*peering at the card table*)   Can you see a ten of clubs anywhere, Mr Roget, or am I going blind?

Roget   I'm sorry?

Fenwick   (*not looking up*)   Wondering what?

Roget   Well, whilst I was cataloguing your collection, it occurred to me that a cross-referencing system might render it more accessible. A link perhaps, not only between the artefacts, but between categories, in accordance with their differing provenance and varying uses, both real and symbolic. Egyptian amulets, for example, of which you have several, might be located under the heading Egypt – obviously – but also under Religion, or Votive Objects, or indeed Insects in the case of scarabs –

Fenwick   Are you volunteering for this thankless task, Roget?

Roget   Well, I –

Harriet, **Maria** *and* **Isobel** *come in, breathlessly.* **Harriet** *is dressed as Britannia,* **Maria** *as a shepherdess, with crook etc. A reluctant* **Isobel** *brings up the rear, dressed as a sheep.*

Harriet   They've just put a brick through the greenhouses, Papa.

Fenwick *doesn't look up.*

Fenwick   I'm sure they didn't mean it.

Susannah   Take a leaf out of your father's book, Harriet. View it with sublime equanimity. You see in his eyes, it is not a brick, not at all, but more a sort of proletarian calling card.

Maria   They're setting carts on fire. The poor horses are screeching with panic.

Fenwick   It will all blow over presently, Maria.

Harriet   Papa, for goodness sake. They'll tear the house down around our heads.

Fenwick   They wouldn't dream of such a thing, I can assure you –

Harriet   Can't you do something?

Susannah   Yes, Joseph, do something, why don't you –

There is an almighty crash in the distance, and a roar from the mob.

Fenwick   What do you suggest?

Harriet   I don't know. Talk to them. They'll listen to you. Calm them before they burn the house down.

Fenwick   They know I'm on their side, they won't touch us.

Susannah   All this hoo-hah about corn –

Fenwick   Fish. Corn was last week.

Susannah   Always on the side of the mob, I don't understand it. It's pure, what's the word I'm looking for –

Fenwick   Perhaps you'd prefer them to burn the house down.

Susannah   Pure affectation, don't you think so, Mr Armstrong?

Fenwick *puts down his pen.*

Fenwick   We are trying to work, Susannah. Do you mind?

Susannah   Good God. I have your attention. What did I do?

Harriet   Accused him of affectation and you know how he loathes anything quite so overtly bourgeois.

There is another roar and a crash.

Maria   Go and talk to them, Father, please!

Fenwick   Maria. A riot is like a play. Action, reversal, climax, catharsis and we all go home. A relief, generally speaking, in a play. Disappointing in a riot, but true nevertheless.

The noise dies down slightly.

Isobel   I think they're moving off, sir.

They all listen. Another crash of glass, another louder roar.

Susannah   There go the cucumber frames.

Fenwick   Let us hope that's the catharsis. They'll all trail home soon, tired but happy. Twopence off fish and that's all they want. We demand our rights as Englishmen, we demand that herrings be less expensive. Universal suffrage? Not interested. Revolution? Bugger it. We demand fish. No one dreams of taking over the fishmongers. Not a revolutionary amongst them.

Susannah   Thank God.

He turns back to his desk.

Harriet   You said you wanted to see a rehearsal of our play, Papa. And I'd rather like to get it over with.

Fenwick (*reading*)   'Gentlemen of the Newcastle Literary and Philosophical Society, Ladies, we stand on the cusp' – (*He pauses, considers, scratches out and replaces words.*) 'threshold' – 'the very brink' – no, that sounds ominous. Cusp or threshold then, which d'you prefer?

Harriet   I don't know, cusp. So can we show you our play? Mama says we would benefit from your advice and criticism.

Fenwick   When have you ever taken my advice, Harriet? And as for criticism, the last time I dared to utter mild dissent you threw a pot of tea at me.

Fenwick *turns back to his desk.* **Maria** *gives a twirl.*

Maria   What do you think, Mr Roget?

Roget   Sorry? Oh, I see, very, yes, most . . . affecting.

Fenwick   Cusp? Doesn't sound right to me somehow.

Maria   I'm playing an Arcadian Idyll.

Armstrong   We guessed immediately.

Harriet   It's metaphorical.

Armstrong   Oh, obviously.

Maria It was Harriet's idea.

Susannah Harriet is an uncommon genius, Mr Armstrong, to read her poetry is to be reminded of, oh, Milton, Shakespeare, Southey, that other fellow, you name it, you must show the gentlemen your poems, Harriet, no point them languishing in a drawer –

Harriet Mama, please –

Susannah But they're such pretty little verses, dear –

Harriet Do we have to talk about them, Mama?

Roget I'm sure they're very fine, but perhaps Miss Fenwick prefers to hide her light at present. Very understandable.

Harriet Thank you, Mr Roget.

Armstrong What's the plot to this entertainment then?

Maria I'm sorry?

Armstrong Your play. Is it comedy or tragedy?

Maria How would you describe the plot to our play, Harriet?

Harriet It's a hymn to progress.

Roget How apt.

Maria Of course when we say hymn, we don't mean it literally –

Harriet They're not completely stupid, Maria –

Maria Because in any case Harriet has rejected established religion, haven't you, Harriet –

Armstrong Very wise.

Harriet Maria represents the past, and I represent the future.

Roget Arcadia meets Britannia, very neat.

Harriet I am Empire, Industry, Science, Wealth and Reason.

Maria　For the most part I sit on a hillock and wave at my flock. According to Harriet, this suggests Pastoral Innocence –

Harriet　I think the gentlemen have grasped the general principle, Maria –

Maria　I must say it's terribly dull, I don't know how those poor shepherdesses stood it.

Harriet　I plan to have a sort of chimney, here, as a headpiece, but the steam is proving a little complicated at present.

Roget　I see. We look forward to that. But tell me, I'm interested in your idea of pastoral innocence. Where does it come from?

Harriet　I don't quite catch your drift.

Roget　Shepherding's a harsh trade. Living in this region you cannot fail to have noticed that. Bo Peep might freeze to death on these hillsides. Drifts ten feet deep on the Cheviots last year, and no sign of spring until May. Hardly an Arcadian Idyll.

Harriet　Maria represents an ideal. That's what idyll means, Mr Roget.

Roget　Of course. But is this ideal based on truth? Does an idyll have its basis in reality?

Harriet　Yes. No. You are being very difficult.

Armstrong　Leave her alone, Roget.

Harriet　It's a fable. Our play is a fable. And that's a sort of universal truth.

Armstrong　Of course it is.

Harriet　You're even more irritating than Mr Roget. He at least resists the temptation to partronise.

Armstrong　I'm sorry. Forgive me. No doubt all will be

revealed when we see the performance.

Harriet   Exactly.

Susannah   It's best not to cross her, Mr Armstrong. She's as stubborn as her father.

Armstrong   Yes, I can see that.

Susannah   But sweet, sweet –

Harriet *glares.*

Roget   So. Anyway. I'm sure the play will be a delight. Isobel, you're obviously playing . . . what?

Isobel   A sheep, sir.

Roget   Of course. A sheep. Yes.

Isobel   I've the wrong ears.

Harriet   Oh, for goodness sake, stop complaining about your wretched ears –

Isobel   Sheep don't have ears like this.

Susannah   She's right of course, they don't.

Maria   They're perfectly adequate for a small, unimportant part. No one will notice them, Isobel.

Isobel   To my mind, if you'll excuse me, it's a very low sort of play –

Maria   No one's interested in your mind, dear –

Isobel   – for a start, sheep don't speak.

Harriet   That's the magic of theatre, Isobel. Anything is possible.

Susannah   I had a pet lamb once. Judith. She was a Welsh ewe, and one would almost swear she could speak. Such a plaintive little bleat, of course she's cutlets now, poor thing. Do you bleat, Isobel?

Isobel   My lines are ridiculous. They're infantile. Why can't I say something of consequence?

Harriet Primarily because you're playing a sheep. And besides, some people are not meant to say anything of consequence. As in life, so in a play. Certain rules must be obeyed. And one of them is you stick to your own lines. You can't swap them round as it takes your fancy. Think of the chaos. Think of the audience.

Fenwick What do you think, Isobel? Cusp or threshold?

Isobel It depends on the context, sir. In this instance I think threshold is the word you want. Cusp is too poetic, and also imprecise.

Silence. They all stare at **Isobel**.

Fenwick (*reads*) '. . . we stand on the threshold of a new century, we stand at the gates of a New Jerusalem . . .' Thank you, Isobel.

Harriet Now you've established that, Papa, would you like to see our play or not?

Fenwick I will see it, but not now, Harriet.

Harriet You are impossible, Papa. How many times have we sat through your experiments, your visiting speakers droning endlessly about combustible gases and electricity?

Fenwick You enjoyed every moment of it –

Harriet That's not the point! We've spent hours labelling every piece of your useless bric-a-brac, arranging in alphabetical order your rhinoceros horn, your dried walrus flipper, tooth of hippopotamus, pointless chunks of volcanic lava, even the hair balls of an ox –

Fenwick Calculi they're known as –

Maria He even made us attend the dissection of a dear little spaniel –

Fenwick Which was quite dead, I assure you, gentlemen –

Maria – because he said it would be illuminating –

Susannah You got quite sick, didn't you, dear –

Harriet But you see, Papa, how d'you know our play is not equally illuminating?

Fenwick I've told you, I will watch it, Harriet, but not now –

Harriet *stamps her foot.*

Harriet We have rehearsed and rehearsed the wretched thing because you told us you'd look at it now –

Fenwick Then I'm afraid I must disappoint you.

Harriet You're selfish and cruel and you think of nothing but your own concerns. I hate you.

She storms out.

Susannah Such an awkward age. They can move from sweet docility to murderous rage in the course of a sentence. It's quite unsettling. But just a phase –

Maria It's got nothing to do with her age, Mama. She has a ferocious temper, always has had. I'm not given to rages at all. I'm the quiet one, gentlemen, which is why I have a fiancé and Harriet has not. Excuse me. Harriet, dear . . .

She hurries after **Harriet**.

Isobel Will that be all, sir?

Fenwick Stay a moment, Isobel. Sit down.

Isobel I'd rather not, sir.

Fenwick I'm sorry?

Isobel My back. I cannot sit.

Fenwick You must sit sometimes, surely?

Isobel Yes, sir, but there are occasions when it is painful.

And then it is better that I stand.

Armstrong *goes to her and looks at her twisted back. Takes hold of her.*

Armstrong   Is it getting worse? By that I mean, is the degree of malformation increasingly pronounced?

Isobel   It is a long time since I looked in a glass. But I imagine it is more severe. It feels to be. My clothes twist and pull more.

Armstrong *feels her shoulders and back.*

Armstrong   Does that hurt?

Isobel   The pain is not in my back. It is in my hip.

He moves his hands to her hips, and she jerks away.

There's nothing you can do about it, sir.

Susannah   Quite right, Isobel. They're all quacks. A quart of brandy's what you need for pain, whatever noxious remedy they might prescribe.

Fenwick   Susannah –

Susannah   And don't tell me I'm drunk because I'm not. I'm merely pointing out that physicians never cure anything. That's a well-established fact. None of you know what you're talking about –

Fenwick   And you do I suppose –

Susannah   I don't pretend to –

Fenwick   Can we discuss this later, Susannah –

Susannah   A discussion? With me? How novel. D'you think I'm up to it? Goodness, what shall we have as our topic? 'One Shakespeare is worth ten Isaac Newtons. Discuss.' My dear, I'm in a lather of expectation.

Fenwick   Not half as much as me, I can assure you.

He turns away from her.

I'm sorry you're in pain, Isobel. Are we working you too hard?

Isobel No, sir. The work is not burdensome.

Fenwick You like words, don't you? I've noticed it before.

Isobel I suppose I do, sir.

Fenwick Can you read?

Isobel All Scots can read, sir.

Fenwick I wasn't aware of that.

Isobel It's generally the case, sir.

Armstrong All Scots are born literate, is that what you're saying?

Isobel All Scots learn to read. Most of them anyway.

Fenwick But the English are ignorant?

Isobel I wouldn't go so far as that, sir. Of course I wouldn't.

Fenwick Don't worry, we're not angry with you. But I'm interested in your opinion of the English.

Isobel I don't have any opinion, sir.

Fenwick Be as bold as you please. Is there something you dislike?

Isobel I never said I disliked the English, I merely said that the Scots read a lot of books.

Armstrong You must have some feelings on the subject surely.

Isobel It's hard to say, sir.

Fenwick In what sense?

Isobel I'm not sure what 'English' means. In Scots we have a word for it and it's 'Sassenach'. But they tell me that means only 'Saxon'. And as I'm a lowland Scot, and therefore a Saxon, it seems that I too am a Sassenach.

Roget   So the word has two meanings. The literal and the commonly understood. Perhaps in time, the latter may come to supersede the former, d'you agree?

Isobel   Perhaps, sir. Unfortunately.

Roget   Would you call me English?

Isobel   Yes, sir.

Roget   Even though my father was Swiss?

Susannah   My mother was French and my father grew up in Leitrim. What does that make me?

Fenwick   Isobel?

Isobel   The English are hard to place. Englishness is difficult to pin down. It is like a tide which swallows up everything in its wake, and whilst altered in its constituents, appears outwardly little changed.

Armstrong   Bravo. Who told you that?

Isobel   Why do you assume that I was told it, sir?

Fenwick   So the English are infinitely adaptable and mindlessly rapacious. That's interesting. Are you aware of any other qualities by which we may be identified?

Isobel   Not especially, sir.

Fenwick   None?

Isobel   I only know words, sir. Words are what interest me.

Fenwick   And?

Isobel   The English have a single word, sir, nursery, for the place where both children and plants are raised. Perhaps that is telling. Apart from that, I only know that I am a Scot, sir. I am not one of you.

Fenwick Might that not be class, rather than race,
Isobel?

Isobel I'm sorry, sir, but I find this discussion very
difficult.

Fenwick Why is that?

Isobel Because I'm wearing these ears. You cannot take
me seriously whilst I am disguised as a sheep.

Susannah I think 'disguised' is overstating the case,
Isobel.

Fenwick I'd quite forgotten about the ears actually.

Susannah You see how much attention he pays to a
woman's appearance, gentlemen? Sometimes I think it
hardly worth dressing in the morning.

Harriet *comes in.*

Harriet Papa, there are some men in the kitchen. The
cook has let them in. They say they'd like to 'hide' for a
while.

Susannah *gets up unsteadily.*

Susannah That cook's been drinking again. She opens
the house to anyone after a bottle of brandy. Last week it
was a woman with two pigs, I found them asleep in the
library. I've warned her it must stop. Leave this to me.

She goes. **Fenwick** *gets up.*

Fenwick Susannah, let me deal with this please – excuse
me, gentlemen –

He hurries out after her, followed by **Harriet**.

Harriet (*as she goes*) The men seem quite docile, Papa,
but one of them has a badly sliced head . . .

Isobel *is left with* **Roget** *and* **Armstrong**.

Isobel May I go now?

Roget Of course, Isobel.

Armstrong No, stay a while. Tell us about yourself.

Isobel I'm sorry, sir?

Armstrong Tell us about your life.

Isobel Why would you want me to do that, sir?

Armstrong It might be interesting.

Isobel It's not.

Roget Let her go, Armstrong.

Armstrong You're rather pretty, d'you know that, Isobel?

Roget Armstrong –

Armstrong I don't suppose anyone's ever told you that before have they, Isobel?

Isobel Only a blind man or a liar would say such a thing, sir.

Armstrong You think me a liar?

Isobel I won't tell you what I think of you.

Armstrong You're a pretty woman, accept the fact.

Isobel I know what I am. I am a serving girl, a waiting woman, a maid, hireling, drudge and skivvy. I am a lackey, an underling, a menial and a minion. I am all these things but I am not pretty.

Roget A general factotum.

Isobel A slave.

Roget A retainer perhaps?

Isobel A dogsbody.

Roget *laughs.*

Isobel I know twenty-seven words for what I am, sir.

And none of them corresponds to pretty.

Roget   Twenty-seven words for servant, that's remarkable, but yes I suppose it's possible –

Armstrong   Beauty is more complex than mere appearance, Isobel.

Roget   And of course there are different catagories of servant, aren't there? What about amanuensis? Slightly more democratic but certainly a possibility – I presume you're only counting the female variants, are you –

Armstrong   I wish you'd take me seriously, Isobel.

Roget   We're trying to have a discussion, Armstrong –

Isobel   I believe you're making fun of me, sir.

Armstrong   I swear on my life, I am not –

Isobel   And I would ask you to stop –

Armstrong   Very well. It seems I can't persuade you. I wish I could.

Isobel   May I go now, sir?

Roget   Of course you may, and please believe me, Mr Armstrong means no harm, I can assure you – What about scullion – did you count that?

Isobel   I did, sir. Thank you, sir. If that's all, I will go now.

She hurries out.

Roget   Pretty?

Armstrong   She loves it. Every woman loves a compliment. Especially a plain one.

Roget   You're toying with her. It's cruel beyond belief.

Armstrong   No, I'm not actually. I don't find her plain at all. I find her quite fascinating.

He pours himself a glass of brandy.

A strange little thing, isn't she? I wonder . . .

Roget   What?

Armstrong   I wonder what caused the hump . . .

He sips his brandy thoughtfully. Blackout.

Fade up dim lighting. English pastoral music in background. **Maria**
enters during the scene change, and reads out a letter from **Edward**.

Maria   'My dear Maria, A chapati is a sort of thin,
flapping bread, since you ask. This morning on rising, I
found a fierce boil beneath my ear, the size of a gull's egg.
The boy wanted to apply some sort of dung to it, but as
he was loathe to divulge which animal it might originate
from I declined his offer. I am in great agony. Yesterday
one of our bearers was crushed by an elephant. His head
popped open like a pomegranate. So now we are one
bearer short, and the remaining are in a very sullen mood.
We visited some of their temples on Saturday, and were all
agreed that many of the statues are quite disgraceful. The
Collector said it makes one wonder what sort of jinks they
get up to when they are out of our jurisdiction. A Miss
Cholmondely, out on a visit from Yorkshire, quite fainted
away from shock at the sight of one of them. We had done
our utmost to preserve her from the spectacle, but she
would insist. Whereas gentlemen are able to appreciate the
instructional aspect of such things, women, for the most
part, are merely affronted, or, as in the case of Miss
Cholmondely, quite prostrated. Afterwards, she remembered
nothing of the incident, or indeed the statues, which is a
blessing. The natives seemed to find the episode faintly
entertaining. Their temperament is generally placid, I find,
but not in the English manner. An Englishman has a
modesty of demeanour, a judicious thoughtfulness and an
equanimity of temperament which makes him a stranger to
passionate outbursts. The native composure is altogether
different. One might almost feel that they were hiding
something. Please write soon. Your affectionate servant,
Edward.'

Scene Two

Lights up. Same room, 1999.

The stage is now almost bare apart from the desk, now free of its clutter, and a one-bar electric fire which glows weakly. A single electric light bulb casts a thin light. Tea chests are scattered round the room, some full, some still in the process of being packed. Piles of books and clothes. **Ellen** *is sorting through stuff and packing it up.* **Kate***, wearing scarves and a coat, is talking on her mobile phone.*

Kate   ... no, she's sitting here in front of me ... yes I'll tell her ... she hasn't had time to sit down and think about it, that's all ... no honestly, I don't foresee any problems at all ... OK ... bye, Mike.

She clicks off the phone.

He says they have to know by New Year's Eve.

Ellen *carries on packing.*

Ellen   Yes, OK.

Kate   I just think it's a wonderful opportunity, that's all.

Ellen   Yes. I know.

Pause.

Kate   So have you talked to Tom about it?

Ellen   Sort of. Look, I'll sort it out, OK –

Phil *comes in carrying clipboards, tape measures etc.*

Phil   D'you mind if I take a few measurements in here?

Ellen   No, no of course not. Kate, this is Phil, he's doing a building survey.

Kate   I think I'll go and make some tea, it's bloody freezing in here.

She goes out. **Phil** *looks slightly awkward.*

Phil   Did I interrupt something?

Ellen   Not at all. Kate's an old colleague of mine. She staying with us for New Year but I think the cold's getting to her.

Phil *takes out his tape measure and looks round the room.*

Phil   By, it's a canny size, this place.

Ellen   That's why we have to sell it. It's crippling us. I got it from my mum. Her parents had it before her. But we can't afford it so that's that.

She looks at her watch.

What exactly is Tom doing in the basement?

Phil   Showing us where the pipes run under the floors. They've got to come up. Most of them are lead. I'm surprised you've not been poisoned. You wouldn't believe what you find when you start poking around the found-ations of some of these old houses. We were sorting out a place in Corbridge last year and we found a Roman bathhouse. Well, they said it was Roman. Which was a bit of a blow, like, because I fancied a few of the tiles for our kitchen, but with it being that old they slapped a preservation order on it.

Ellen   What's the plan for this room, then?

Phil   Corporate hospitality. Private bar in here, private conference facilities through there, private gym. Private sauna for the Scandinavians. Good views of the park, handy for the miniature railway in case any of them are steam train enthusiasts –

Ellen   A miniature railway?

Phil   Actually, they call it a heritage railway.

Ellen   They told us they just wanted to restore it to its former glory.

Phil   Aye, but everything has to be on a heritage trail now and you can't be on a heritage trail unless you've got attractions. I mean, this is a nice enough house and that, but it's not got much going for it in your commercial sense. People like to feel they're getting their money's worth. I think they want to reopen one of the mines down the road as well. You know. Employ some ex-miners to dress up as miners and pretend to dig coal and then charge people a tenner to go down and experience life at the coal face.

Ellen   You're not serious?

Phil   Well, why not? They've Disneyfied everything else, why should the miners get off scot-free?

Ellen   It's such ... what's the word I'm looking for.

Phil   Shite.

Ellen   I mean, why fill it with ersatz history when it's already got a proper history? It doesn't need to be ponsified and half-timbered. The Newcastle Lit and Phil had its first meetings in this room, did you know that?

Phil   I didn't, no –

Ellen   Lavoisier visited this house –

Phil   Oh aye, who's he then?

Ellen   He discovered that combustion is a process in which oxygen combines with another substance. Up till then they thought the combustible ingredient was something called phlogiston.

Phil   Bit of a comedian then.

Ellen   Tom Paine was given secret readings in this very room. It's a big, plain, solid house, it's not quaint or charming. The history of this house is the history of radicalism and dissent and intellectual enquiry, and they're going to turn it into a tin of souvenir biscuits.

Phil   Well, don't sell it then.

Ellen   I told you. We can't afford it. Tom's been made redundant, and it just eats up money –

Phil   Is he in the same line of business as you then?

Kate　No. He's an English lecturer.

Phil　Actually, I meant to ask you something, seeing as I'm here like. My seven-year-old daughter, we think she's allergic to jam. Big red hives on her arms every time she eats it. And I wondered if it was common, like. A jam allergy.

Ellen　I've no idea. I would have thought it was some additive rather than the jam itself.

Phil　You don't see many cases of it then?

Ellen　Oh, I see, no, I'm sorry, I'm not a medical doctor, I'm a research scientist.

Phil　So you're not a doctor?

Ellen　Yes. But not a medical one.

Phil　Oh.

Pause.

So you don't know anything about medicine then?

Ellen　No.

Phil　What, nothing at all?

Ellen　Not in any helpful way, no. I'm sorry.

Phil　You must know a bit, like, being a scientist.

Ellen　I don't actually.

Phil　I bet you do really.

Ellen　No I don't, honestly.

Phil　So what d'you do then?

Ellen　I'm sorry?

Phil　What d'you research?

Ellen　Oh, it's boring.

Phil　Why d'you do it then?

Ellen Well, not to me. It's not boring to me.

He taps the floor, gets down on his knees, jots notes down on his clipboard.

Phil I tell you something, black holes, I like the sound of them, it's like the bloody *X-Files*. Apparently, light goes into them, right, but it never comes out again, and if you're hanging around on the edge of one, time slows down until you get to the horizon and then it stops altogether. They're like sort of wormholes, right, and if we could go down one of these wormholes we'd come out in a different universe. Incredible. Now I wouldn't mind researching them. Mind you, I suppose you'd need the qualifications.

Ellen I don't know much about any of that, I'm afraid. Not really my area.

Phil So what is your area then?

Ellen I'm doing . . . well, I work in genetics, that sort of thing.

She looks at her watch again.

I wish Tom'd hurry up, he's been down there for ages.

Phil Cloning, is that the sort of thing?

Ellen No no, nothing like that.

Phil I bet it is.

Ellen No, it's not.

Phil Actually, I've always wanted to ask a scientist this: what d'you make of spontaneous combustion?

Ellen I'm sorry?

Phil Because a mate of mine said a friend of his found the lad next door fried to crisp, well, a pile of ashes actually, apart from his slippers, which he said were just sitting there, smouldering. With the feet still in them. Not a mark on them, he said. Apparently it's very common.

Ellen It is?

Phil   So what d'you make of that then?

Ellen   Well, I'm not sure. I think it's probably an urban myth.

Phil   You see, that's the sort of science that interests me. The tricky stuff.

Ellen   Well, it's certainly . . . that.

Phil   What about alien invasions then? D'you think we're being visited by extraterrestrials?

Ellen   Er, I don't think so, no.

Phil   Now, no disrespect, don't get me wrong, but that's what I hate about scientists. Closed minds.

Ellen   Oh. Sorry.

Phil   So why don't you believe in them?

Ellen   It's not a matter of belief. It's a matter of evidence, and I don't have any that persuades me they exist.

Phil   I don't know how you can be so sure –

Ellen   I'm not sure. If someone can present me with compelling evidence of their existence, I'll accept it –

Phil   Well, a friend of mine, right, said him and his wife were followed home from the races one day by a lozenge-shaped thing, a bit like a Victory V but green, sort of hovering and swooping, just above the hedge. Followed them for twenty mile. And then shot off in the direction of the power station. And this lad works for the council, so you couldn't call him a nutter.

Ellen   Is this the same one who found the smouldering slippers?

Phil   No, that was his mate. So you see, you say you've got no evidence and I've just given you two very compelling bits of it if you ask me.

Ellen   Anecdotal doesn't count. They could be making it up. Or elaborating something much more explicable.

Phil   Why would they want to do that?

Ellen   Because people like telling stories. They like sitting around and telling tales for which there's no rational explanation. Like ghost stories. And crop circles. And being a reincarnation of Marie Antoinette. I'm not entirely sure why. You'd need to ask a psychologist.

Phil   Well, I know what I think, and I think we'll have to agree to disagree on this one.

Ellen   Fair enough.

Phil   Mind you. This cloning lark. I bet that could get a bit out of hand, couldn't it?

Ellen   In what way?

Phil   Well, it'll be people next, everyone knows that, I mean, they say it won't but it will. And what worries me is, well, can you imagine, I mean, say if, I don't know, William Hague decided to clone himself. There'd be two of him then. Or hundreds even. Imagine that.

Ellen   I can't see why he'd want to clone himself. What's in it for him? And even if he did, you wouldn't get hundreds of William Hagues. They'd be genetically identical, but culturally and socially and chronologically completely different.

Phil   Well, you say that . . .

Ellen   It's true –

Phil   No, but just imagine it for a minute. William Hague looks like something that needs to be put back in the oven, right?

Ellen   No he doesn't –

Phil   He does, man. He looks like he's not cooked properly. D'you remember Pilsbury Dough men? You got them in little tins. He looks like one of them. And if there was hundreds of him, quite apart from the politics, which'd be very fucking scary, it'd be like a science-fiction film,

Invasion of the Pastry People –

Ellen   Yes, well, that's science fiction, not science –

Phil   Well, the whole thing's very dodgy, you don't know what you're dabbling in, if you ask me. I think I'll stick to rewiring. That's as far as my technological know-how goes.

Ellen   Probably just as useful as what I do.

Phil   You still haven't told me exactly what that is.

Ellen   Foetal diagnostics. Detecting genetic abnormalities in the foetus. Well, attempting to anyway.

Phil   I thought you said it was nothing to do with cloning?

Ellen   It isn't –

Phil   It's as close as makes no difference –

Ellen   It's very complicated –

Phil   Oh aye.

Ellen   I'm sorry. I'm not used to talking about my work, OK? People get the wrong end of the stick. They get very angry and accuse me of all sorts of things, and mostly they haven't a clue what they're talking about –

Kate *appears with a tray of tea and a bottle of whiskey.*

Kate   Hi. Hot toddies all round, and if you think it's cold in here, try the kitchen. I don't know how you live here.

Ellen   You get used to it.

Phil   So what's your opinion on spontaneous combustion then, Kate?

Kate   I'm sorry?

Ellen   Phil has a friend of a friend of a friend who burst into flames.

Kate   Oh, that. Absolute bollocks. Are you having your tea straight or with a shot of this?

Phil *looks at his watch.*

Phil Well . . .

She slugs whiskey into his mug and hands it to him.

Kate It's after five, and it's starting to snow out there. Give yourself a break. Ellen?

Phil What d'you mean it's bollocks? It's very well documented actually –

Ellen Did you know they want to turn the house into a theme park?

Kate So don't let them. Don't sell it. You don't have to.

Ellen If it were that straightforward –

Kate It is.

She hands her a mug of tea. Pause.

Ellen Kate's company are offering me a job, Phil, which will pay me a great deal of money, which might even mean we can pull out of selling the house, and I'm not sure whether to take it.

Phil So what's the problem?

Kate That's what I keep saying.

Ellen It's not just my decision, it's Tom's too –

Kate I don't know what it's got to do with Tom.

Ellen Well, he's my husband, that's one consideration –

Kate But what exactly is he objecting to?

Ellen Nothing. He's not objecting to anything.

Kate Then I don't see what the dilemma is –

Ellen No, you wouldn't.

Kate What's that supposed to mean?

Ellen You're fifteen years younger than me and nothing frightens you. You still want to be God.

Kate   Christ, you do talk shite sometimes.

Ellen   You're still in love with the work –

Kate   So are you –

Ellen   But with me it's been a long marriage and some of the romance has worn off –

Phil   If you don't mind me asking, what is this job?

Kate   Ellen is a very brilliant scientist, did she tell you that?

Phil   I'm sure she is. In her own field.

Ellen   Phil believes in flying saucers.

Phil   That's not what I said actually. But you're being very cagey about this job. You see, that's why people don't trust scientists. They're always up to something.

Ellen   I'm having an ethical crisis, Phil –

Phil   What did I tell you? I knew it was dodgy –

Tom (*off*)   Ellen?

Ellen   We're up here.

Kate   Ethical crisis, for fuck's sake –

Ellen   The fact that you've never had a moral qualm in your life doesn't mean you have superior reasoning power, it just means you have a limited imagination –

Kate   Have you got children, Phil?

Phil   Two. Boy and a girl.

Kate   If, very very early in your wife's pregnancy, you were able to discover in your child the gene for, say, Alzheimer's disease, or asthma, or maybe something more alarming like schizophrenia, would you be grateful for that information?

Phil   Er . . . I'm not sure.

Kate   Ellen's team have perfected a technique that does

this. It's completely safe, and it can be done very very
early. And the most important thing is it's non-invasive, so
there's no risk to the foetus. It's pretty radical stuff.
Wouldn't you say this was a good thing?

Phil   Aye, I suppose so.

Kate   And my company want her to come and work for
us because we can invest a lot of money in its development, so that eventually, it'll be available to a mass-market.
Everyone benefits, nobody suffers. Can you see a problem
with that, Phil?

Phil   I can actually.

Ellen   You can?

Phil   Aye. What's the point of it?

Kate   Well, you might want to terminate the pregnancy,
for example.

Phil   What, because the kid might get asthma?

Kate   Well, not for something like that, obviously.

Phil   One of mine's got asthma, allergies, the lot. Loads of
kids round us have got them. I think it's the pollution, me.

Kate   But if it was manic depression for example? Or
schizophrenia?

Phil   My uncle Stan was manic depressive and he was
magic. He built us a tree house covered in shells and bits
of coloured glass. He used to play the Northumbrian pipes.

Ellen   We're mapping the human gene system at the
moment. There's something called the Human Genome
Project. Have you heard of it?

Phil   You what?

Kate   It's incredibly exciting, it's like a new map of
humanity, every element described and understood. I mean,
it's breathtaking –

Phil   Oh aye.

Kate We'll be able to pinpoint genes for particular types of cancer, for neurological disorders, for all sorts of things, some of them benign, some of them not, but what it really means is we'll understand the shape and complexity of a human being, we'll be able to say this is a man, this is exactly who he is, this is his potential, these are his possible limitations. And manic depression is genetic. We'll pin it down soon.

Phil And then what? No more Uncle Stans.

Kate I think you're probably being very romantic about him. I mean, where is he now?

Phil He's dead.

Kate What happened to him?

Phil He killed himself.

Kate Exactly.

Phil You never met him. You don't know anything about what went on in his life, or what things meant to him –

Kate I'm just saying manic depression can be fatal –

Phil Bollocks, man, you don't know what you're talking about –

Tom *comes in, in thick outdoor clothes. He looks white and shaky.* **Kate** *beams at him.*

Kate Tom. Hi. D'you want whiskey with your tea?

Tom What? Oh ... um ... yes ... yes, please ...

Ellen Is something wrong?

Tom Yes ... yes, I suppose there is ...

Ellen Well what?

Tom We've found something a bit odd underneath one of the kitchen cupboards. In the extension.

Phil If it's the electrics, I could have told you that. Whoever did your wiring was a bloody menace.

Tom No, no. It's a box of um . . . it's a box of bones.

Blackout. Music.

Maria *comes on with a letter which she reads in a pool of light during the scene change.*

Maria 'My dear Maria, I hope you are well. My neck had subsided, but now my gums feel all wrong. They are white at the edges and bleed when I eat. Please send one bottle Daffy's Elixir and two of Spilsbury's Efficacious Drops by return of post. Yesterday the Collector's horse was bitten by a snake, and one of our party beat it to death with an ivory club. The snake, not the horse. It was an enormous size, and the sight of it made me long quite childishly for our own gentle land, where one can walk a country road without being threatened by vicious nature on all sides. Do English animals kill? I can think of none. One never feels apprehensive about sheep, for instance, or cattle. Bulls can be unpredictable, of course. I dream of home, and yet I must own that my dreams are strangely imprecise. The mere word, "England" conjures up a landscape in my head, and though this picture is familiar, it is not a place I have ever visited, but rather *almost* such a place. It is unbearably hot here, and though I stay indoors a great deal, I cannot think that such extremes are good for ones general health. I think of you often, in the cooler, gentler landscape of home, and I am glad that you are safe and far from harm and strife. Your most affectionate servant, Edward.'

Scene Three

Lights up.

1799. One day later.

The dining-room. A large table centre stage. Chairs around it. Chandelier. **Isobel** *is polishing the table.* **Roget** *comes in, wrapped up in coat and scarves.*

Roget Isobel?

Isobel *turns. She looks disappointed.*

Isobel   Oh. Mr Roget.

Roget   Sorry. Were you expecting someone else?

Isobel   No, sir.

Roget   I was looking for Dr Fenwick.

Isobel   He's not here, sir.

Roget   No.

Uneasy pause.

I was wondering, Isobel, whether you'd care to take a stroll with me later today.

Isobel   No thank you, sir.

Roget   Oh.

Awkward pause.

Perhaps I'll just wait here for Dr Fenwick then.

He goes to the window.

Awful weather.

Pause.

Isobel   Yes, sir.

Silence.

Roget   I'm afraid I can't get used to the northern climate. Can't seem to get warm. In Edinburgh I was chilled to the marrow, even in summer. That terrible wind off the sea. And the same here. Relentless, unforgiving cold. All year round.

Isobel   Perhaps you should go back to London if you can't stand the climate.

Roget *looks at her.*

Isobel   I didn't mean to offend you, sir.

Roget   No offence taken. Slavey. I thought of that in the night.

She looks at him.

Roget   Another word for servant.

Isobel   I counted that.

Roget   Did you count Scots dialect words?

Isobel   Some. D'you have a particular interest in the word servant, sir?

Roget   It's not the word itself that interests me. I just like lists. How are we to understand the world unless we organise it coherently? The world is a web of connections and affinities, don't you think? I have a systematic mind. I get it from my mother. You should see her household accounts. The cross-referencing would stump a mathematician. I'm a good physician because I'm methodical and intermittently inspired.

Isobel *is silent.*

Roget   Have you tried laughing gas?

Isobel   No, sir.

Roget   I thought Dr Fenwick may have offered you some. We once thought it might cure consumption but it all proved rather inconclusive. It has a remarkably pleasant effect though, I can thoroughly recommend it as a tonic –

Fenwick *comes in, with* **Susannah**.

Fenwick   What are you doing, Roget?

Roget   Waiting for you, sir.

Susannah   Isobel, the table is quite polished enough. We don't want to be blinded over supper.

Isobel *hesitates.*

Susannah   Off you go, stop dithering.

Isobel   Yes, madam.

She goes. **Susannah** *settles down to some needlework.*

Fenwick   Not putting ideas in her head, were you?

Roget   What about?

Fenwick   I don't know. You tell me.

Roget   We were talking about words.

Fenwick   I've seen girls like her ruined, that's all. Taken advantage of. Men think they're game for anything because no one will marry them. And I don't want her ruined, I don't want her heart broken, d'you understand me?

Susannah   So noble of you.

Roget   I had no intention of ruining her.

Fenwick   We have an enlightened view of servants in this household. We think of them as family –

Susannah   Of course you don't Joseph, you like to think that, but you don't really –

Fenwick (*ignoring her*)   – and you don't fuck your family. Whatever they might do in some of the more remote areas. Now, to the point. I want you to look out of this window. What do you see?

Roget *goes and looks, uncertain of what is required of him.*

Roget   Um . . . A view . . . A vista? . . . A prospect?

Fenwick   Specifically, Roget, specifically.

Roget   A city landscape . . . An urban panorama?

Fenwick   It's not a word game, Roget. An urban panorama composed of what?

Roget *looks again.*

Roget   Oh. I see. Banks running down to the Tyne, sir. The bridge. Smoke curling into the frozen air. Ships. Coal barges.

Fenwick   D'you know what I see? Bridges. Plural. Can you imagine?

Roget   Bridges, plural . . . Well, yes, I think I can imagine that.

Fenwick   Huge, graceful bridges. Triumphs of engineering. Hymns to invention and the conquest of nature.

Roget   I see.

Fenwick   You don't sound inspired.

Susannah   That's because he's not, Joseph.

Roget   Well, yes, bridges. There's no doubt, that would be a very good thing.

Fenwick   This is a great city, Roget. It could be the Athens of the North.

Roget   I understand Edinburgh has already claimed that particular title, sir.

Fenwick   Bugger Edinburgh. You know who lived here in the sixties? You know who chose to make Newcastle his home? No less a man than –

Roget/Susannah (*together*)   – Jean Paul Marat –

Roget   You told me.

Fenwick   Of course what he was doing practising as a vet is beyond me. No feel for it at all. Could kill a creature just by looking at it.

Susannah   That's one skill he took back with him to France then.

Fenwick   He was great man, Roget. An inspiration. A terrible vet but a great republican.

Roget   Of course it hasn't been huge success in France. Republicanism.

Fenwick   They got rid of the king. That's what the word means for God's sake.

Roget   But at what cost, sir?

Susannah   My husband doesn't like to sully himself with such vulgarities as cost, Roget –

Fenwick   We'll do it differently here. It may take longer, but I guarantee you, one hundred years from now, there will be no monarchy in England –

Susannah   Take my advice, Mr Roget, and stop him before he starts –

Fenwick (*ignoring her*)   – and how will we get there? By the relentless, irresistible advance of science and the consequent wider dissemination of knowledge.

Roget   Dr Guillotine managed to dispatch the king quite effectively purely by the application of science. Are you planning something similar here?

Fenwick   The monarchy will disappear, Roget, it's inevitable. Logic demands it. Science is inextricably linked with democracy. Once people are released from their ignorance, they will demand universal suffrage, and once we have it, it follows as night follows day that we will vote the monarchy out of existence.

Roget   How do you propose to achieve this spectacular release from bondage?

Fenwick   By the end of the nineteenth century everyone will understand how the world works. By the end of the following century, if you can imagine that far, every man or woman in the street will understand more than we can ever dream of. Electricity, the stars, the composition of the blood, complexities beyond our imagination, will be as easily understood as the alphabet. Magic and superstition won't come into it. And it stands to reason, any citizen with the facts at his disposal could not tolerate a monarchical system unless he was mentally impaired or wilfully resistant to reality.

Roget   It seems to be a condition of existence to resist an idea of reality when it threatens a tradition of mystery.

People like the monarchy because it's got nothing to do with reality.

Fenwick Oh, they bang on and on about our mystical, pageant-filled past, and I say bugger it, it's a myth. The British monarchy doesn't bear too much close scrutiny, Roget, let me tell you.

Susannah I feel sorry them, poor creatures. So much responsibility, so much money, and so badly dressed. The last time I saw the queen she looked like a catastrophe in a cake shop –

Fenwick Susannah, what exactly are you doing here?

Susannah I'm sewing.

Fenwick Is there any need for you to do it here? Why are you following me around the house?

Susannah For the simple reason that if I didn't, you'd forget I existed.

Fenwick Don't be ridiculous –

Susannah He doesn't listen to me, have you noticed, Mr Roget? I said, Joseph, that I pitied the king and queen. They are mere mortals, like the rest of us.

Fenwick The Hanoverians are, to a man, philistine, dull and profoundly stupid, not to mention vulgar.

Susannah Exactly. Just like the rest of us. That's precisely why they're popular, Joseph.

Fenwick But deep down, people still suspect that when the king farts he farts stardust. On the other hand, if they're just like us, why don't they live like us, why are we keeping them in palaces? At a time when our people cannot afford to feed themselves adequately, when children sleep in the streets with vermin for company, we still think it reasonable to fund a drab family of feuding Germans who do nothing more than wave at us from their carriages occasionally. Ask yourself this simple question, Roget. Are we all mad?

Susannah   Note, again, Mr Roget, how he addresses his question to you, rather than to me –

Fenwick   Susannah, in God's name, stop interrupting me –

Susannah   I'm sorry if I exasperate you, Joseph, but I prefer it to being ignored. Excuse me.

She throws down her needlework and goes out, furious. Silence.

Fenwick   Sorry about that, Roget. She's er, very highly strung.

Roget   Perhaps she feels – perhaps you –

Fenwick   What?

Roget   Nothing, sir . . . These things are clearly . . . not my affair . . .

Awkward pause.

Fenwick   Where were we?

Roget   You were being dangerously seditious.

Fenwick   Not that you'd dream of turning me in.

Roget   So science is what, as far as you're concerned? A sort of philanthropic odyssey? Its sole purpose to rescue people from ignorance and dissolve the state?

Fenwick   We're scientists because we want to change the world.

Roget   We're scientists because we want to understand the world.

Fenwick   We're scientists because we want to change the conditions under which people live.

Roget *says nothing.*

Fenwick   Well. Go on. Argue with me.

Pause.

Roget   Well. I er, I don't think Armstrong would agree

with that at all . . . sir.

Fenwick Fuck Armstrong. What about you?

Roget I . . . I reserve judgement, sir. I take no ethical position. I do what I do because it fascinates me. I don't question its purpose.

Fenwick Piddling niggler.

Pause.

I'm not very keen on Armstrong. I don't suppose that's slipped your notice has it. Only got him here because Farleigh asked me to take him on for three months. Clear eye, sharp brain, ruthless logician. In short, a clever young bastard, but cold of heart.

Roget Does good science require a warm heart?

Fenwick I like to think so, Roget. In fact I suspect pure objectivity is an arrogant fallacy. When we conduct an experiment we bring to bear on it all our human frailties, and all our prejudices, much as we might wish it to be otherwise. I like to think that good science requires us to utilise every aspect of ourselves in pursuit of truth. And sometimes the heart comes into it.

Pause.

I'd better go and find my wife. Excuse me, will you?

Roget Of course.

He goes out. **Roget** *picks up the needlework from the floor and follows him. As they leave by one exit,* **Isobel** *comes in by another, followed by* **Armstrong.** *He takes her hand. She pulls away.*

Armstrong I know you thought my behaviour a little forward yesterday, and I apologise for it, Isobel.

Isobel I accept your apologies, sir. For the third time. Please, no more.

Armstrong However, I must point out that I meant every word. I do think you're very pretty. Is that so odd?

Isobel   It is unusual, sir, that's all.

Armstrong *takes a book from his pocket.*

Armstrong   Will you at least accept this small gift from me?

Isobel   That is not ... it is not necessary, sir.

Armstrong   Oh, reason not the need, Isobel.

Isobel   *King Lear.*

Armstrong   Really? Please, take it, will you?

He tries to hand her the book. She refuses.

So you refuse my present?

Pause. **Isobel** *is confused.*

Isobel   I've never had as gift before, sir.

Armstrong   What, never?

Isobel   I have never, to my recollection, inspired material generosity in others.

Armstrong   Well, in that case, let this be the first time –

He thrusts the book at her. She looks at it.

Isobel   Shakespeare's Sonnets. . . . Oh, sir . . . I am most . . . thank you, sir.

They stand, quietly looking at the book and frozen in time as **Tom** *comes on, wrapped up in outdoor clothes over pyjamas, heavy boots. He has a pair of shears in his hands and an armful of cuttings from the garden.* **Ellen** *enters, dishevelled, in her dressing-gown.*

Ellen   There you are. Where have you been? I woke up and you'd gone.

He doesn't turn round.

Tom   I was just getting some air.

Pause.

I took a few cuttings from the garden. I thought we could

plant them in the new one. Lavender. Honeysuckle. Some of the old white roses. Otherwise it'll all disappear under a car park or something. Roses are all hybrids now. You don't get them like this any more. These ones are older than the century. We should save them.

Ellen What?

Tom The plants. I'm going to have a lot of time for gardening now.

Ellen You'll get another job.

Tom No I won't. You know I won't. I'm too old, I'm too expensive and I don't give a fuck about post-modernism.

Pause. He starts trimming the cuttings.

Ellen I have to give Kate an answer by tomorrow.

Tom So give her one.

Ellen That's what I've been trying to talk to you about.

Tom I know.

Ellen So talk to me.

Tom What is there to say? What do I know about it? What do I know about the esoteric complexities of genetics? Besides, you've made up your mind already –

Ellen Tom, look, I know you're depressed –

Tom I'm not depressed. I'm redundant. And there's a dead body under the kitchen sink.

Ellen It's not a dead body –

Tom That's what it started out as –

Ellen A long time ago –

Tom So what's the difference? At what stage does it stop being disturbing and start being archaeology?

Ellen What did the coroner say?

Tom   The skeleton's small, so she's quite young.

Ellen   She?

Tom   It's a young girl. She's been there since at least the First World War, which is when they extended the kitchen. Where we found her was part of the garden originally. And that's all they told me. You'd think you'd sense something. You'd think something like that would taint the place somehow. I've never felt anything, have you?

Ellen   No, but people don't –

Tom   I do. Remember the house in Coldstream?

Ellen   Yes, but that was just – well, I mean, I don't know, you were in a weird mood.

Tom   No I wasn't. I couldn't go across the threshold because I felt chilled to the marrow. The hairs stood up on the back of my neck.

Ellen   No one else felt that.

Tom   The dog did.

Ellen   So what are you trying to say?

Pause.

Tom   That we've lived with a dead girl under the floor for twenty years. And I find that disturbing. It makes me feel strange. That's all.

Pause.

Ellen   Fine, it makes you feel strange. But to return to more practical matters. The job. Shall I take it or not?

Tom   I can't make the decision for you. I feel responsible, that's what I feel.

Ellen   Sorry?

Tom   For the girl. Now that we've found her.

Ellen   Tom, she's dead, she's been there for years and we've no idea who she is. How can we be responsible for her?

Tom   She was in our house.

Ellen   But we didn't put her there.

Tom   She was a person, she had a name.

Ellen   I know, I'm sorry, look, the thing about the job, they're offering me a lot of money. We need it.

Tom   Rub it in, why don't you.

He sweeps the trimmings into a plastic bag.

Ellen   I just want to know what I have to do to get you to talk about it.

Tom   OK. OK. You've been working on this thing for eight years or something. And now you've got there, you've made the big breakthrough and that's great. What d'you want me to say?

Ellen   Jesus Christ, Tom, I'm not asking you to turn cartwheels, I'm not asking you to put bunting out, I'm asking for advice. I feel like I'm walking on eggshells, I'm frightened to bring the subject up because . . . because . . .

Tom   Because what?

Ellen   In case it offends your self-esteem. Because you've lost your job. And I'm being offered one.

Tom   A, that's ridiculous, and B, it's patronising.

Ellen   Well, what am I supposed to think? I try to talk about it and you just grunt or change the subject or pretend you haven't heard me correctly. Or you read something out of the newspaper that's got nothing to do with anything. It's not my fault, Tom, d'you understand? It's not my fault if work is good for me at the moment, and crap for you. I know things are difficult for you, but stop punishing me for it.

Tom   I'm not punishing you for anything. Surprising though it may seem to you, I actually have concerns beyond the quotidian. I do have thoughts about this job of yours.

Ellen   So why don't you tell me them? I'm not a mind-reader.

Tom   OK. This is the way I look at it. Kate's company's busily mapping the human gene system. Ooh, look there's motor neurone disease. Just nailed cystic fibrosis to the floor. And they look at your work and think, great, we can make money out of this. Eventually, they'll be able to the identify the entire genetic code of any given foetus, is that right?

Ellen   Well, in theory, yes –

Tom   So who's going to be interested in that? Obviously the parents to a certain extent. But who's really going to want this information? Insurance companies. Mortgage lenders. Private health companies. Employers. All I'm saying is it's complicated. In the hands of people who don't understand it properly, which is most of the above, it'll be something else to judge people by and discriminate with. What starts off as something with all the forces of good behind it, will be swallowed up by the market-place. In which, as you know, I have little faith. Something about the idea of perfectibility disturbs me, but it obviously excites some people. They'll want to buy it. Everyone will want a piece of it, but you'll only get it if you're rich, or somehow deemed deserving by people who've never had a complex thought in their lives, and think ethics is a branch of interior design.

Ellen   So what's your solution? Not everyone can benefit from it, it might be controlled by nasty capitalists, so let's not bother?

Tom   I don't think that, no . . .

Ellen   But you don't actually have a solution, do you?

Tom   No. I'm just saying you don't either.

He clears up the rest of the mess.

Did I tell you there was a tiny gold chain there?

Ellen Sorry?

Tom With the body. The coroner found it.

He picks up his cuttings and bag.

Right. Rooting powder. I bet we haven't got any.

He goes out. She follows him.

Ellen Tom –

Isobel *shuts the book.*

Isobel I'll take great care of it, sir. It's beautiful.

Armstrong Why did you agree to meet me today?

Isobel I'm not sure. I think perhaps it was the novelty. No man has ever asked such thing of me.

Armstrong Surely that can't be true. What about at home, in Scotland?

Isobel Do not ask me to talk about myself.

Armstrong Why not?

Isobel I'm unused to answering questions. When I talk about myself my face feels hot. When I talk about myself I feel that I am lying.

Armstrong Are you?

Isobel I'm not sure. I try not to. But we all lie about ourselves.

Armstrong Do we?

Isobel We don't mean to but we do.

Armstrong Do you lie in general?

Isobel No. Do you?

Armstrong Inconsequentially.

He kisses her. She is taken by surprise, and pulls away.

Armstrong Don't you trust me?

Isobel I do not know you, sir.

Armstrong You've allowed me to kiss you. What does that mean?

Isobel That I am susceptible to flattery.

Armstrong So you don't trust me?

Isobel No, sir.

Armstrong Don't call me sir.

Isobel I would prefer to.

Armstrong My name is Thomas.

Isobel I know that.

Armstrong I kiss you, call you pretty, I give you a book of sonnets. What could be my motive other than genuine affection?

Isobel I have no idea, sir. That is what bothers me. I am confused. Men do not, in general, show such interest in me.

Armstrong You must have been wooed from time to time.

Isobel Once. By an old man with a face like a goat. Perhaps he thought the fact of my hump cancelled out the fact of his face.

Armstrong Will you trust me in time?

Isobel I cannot say, sir.

Armstrong Nevertheless, your face did light up when I appeared in the hallway.

Isobel I was not aware of that.

Armstrong You know it did. You gave me a ravishing smile.

Isobel Now you are most definitely making fun of me.

Armstrong But it is a most beautiful, transforming smile, like sunlight on a glacier –

Isobel Stop it, please. I am not used to such remarks. They do not make me happy, as you no doubt believe, they make me confused –

He takes hold of her, turns her round, covers her twisted back with kisses and caresses, fascinated and bewitched by it.

Armstrong Isobel –

She pulls away, confused.

Isobel Go, sir, you . . . muddle me . . . Leave me, please –

Pause.

Armstrong Very well. If that's what you wish. I'm sorry if I've offended you. My feelings ran away with me. Forgive me. May we meet tomorrow? Please say yes, please.

Isobel Perhaps. I don't know. Perhaps.

He kisses her hand.

Armstrong Till tomorrow then. I have taken the liberty of marking some lines in your book. Look at them, won't you? Page seventy-three.

He goes. **Isobel** *sits down at the table, opens the book at the marked page.*

Isobel (*reading*) 'All days are nights to see till I see thee, All nights bright days when dreams do show me thee.' . . . He thinks my smile ravishing. He thinks it transforming . . . like sunlight on a glacier . . . His name is Thomas . . . Thomas . . .

She stretches round to feel her twisted back. Lights fade.

Act Two

Scene One

Same room as Act One, Scene One.

Maria *comes on in her shepherdess outfit.*

Maria (*reading*) 'My dear Maria, Miss Cholmondely has invited several of us to a party to celebrate the New Year, and I have decided to attend. She plays the harpischord with great skill, and I hear there is to be dancing. Strangely, after all my homesickness, I now feel apprehensive about my return. I know that it is winter in England, and although the heat is oppressive here, one is forced to admit that there is little to recommend a northern English January. Chilblains hold no romance for me. I like the thought of home, but I shiver at what I know to be reality. Last year, two of our lads died of cold, do you remember? We found them in the top meadow, frozen, rigid as stone, clinging together like babes, and were quite unable to prise them apart until we had thawed their corpses before a fire. This memory oppresses me every time I think of England. However, I long to see you, and that is what sustains me. I dream of your soft blue eyes – ' (*She breaks off.*) Blue? My soft blue eyes? Oh, Edward. What are you talking about?

Harriet *and* **Isobel** *come on dressed for their play, clutching pieces of paper on which the script is written.* **Harriet** *begins to move furniture, sets out four chairs.* **Isobel** *and* **Maria** *watch mutely.*

Harriet I hope you've made a start on your lines, Maria. Isobel, for goodness sake, lend a hand, don't just stand there like a, like a –

Isobel – sheep. (*She picks up a chair.*) Where d'you want these?

Harriet   Over here, thank you –

Maria   Harriet, dear, what colour would you call my eyes?

Harriet   I'm sorry?

Maria   Would you call them blue at all?

Harriet   Only if I was utterly unfamiliar with the word. Your eyes are a pronounced and definite brown, Maria. Like mine.

Maria   Are there any conditions of lighting, any curious atmospheric distortions under which they might show themselves to be azure?

Harriet   They are very pleasing as they are, Maria. They will never be blue, and you mustn't wish it.

Maria   Have they ever looked blue to you, Isobel?

Harriet   Oh, for goodness sake –

Isobel   They've never looked blue to me.

Maria   They have always looked brown?

Isobel   Most markedly. It is not a thing one would forget.

Maria   Exactly. That's what I thought.

Fenwick *and* **Susannah** *come in.*

Harriet   No! No! We're not ready –

Fenwick   Oh. Sorry –

Isobel   We're as ready as we're ever going to be.

Susannah   I thought it was just a rehearsal, dear?

Harriet   Oh, very well, come in, sit down, no not there! Here, look where we've set out the chairs.

Maria   I don't think I can perform today. I'm sorry.

Harriet   What?

Maria   I'm afraid I'm not in the humour.

Harriet Excuse me a moment. Maria –

She takes hold of **Maria***'s arm and drags her out, passing* **Armstrong** *and* **Roget** *who enter as they leave.*

Roget Oh. Have we missed it?

Fenwick Unfortunately, no.

Isobel *looks awkward.*

Susannah Still the same ears, I see, Isobel.

Isobel Yes, madam.

Armstrong I think they're very fetching.

Fenwick You're to sit here, I think.

Roget *and* **Armstrong** *sit down next to him.*

Armstrong What's happening?

Susannah One of the actresses is temporarily indisposed.

Fenwick But the actor manager is placating her with the promise of her name appearing most prominently on the handbill, and a solemn vow that Wakefield will not be included in the tour.

Maria *returns, followed by* **Harriet.**

Maria Papa –

Harriet Maria –

Maria Papa, Edward thinks my eyes are blue, he said so in a letter, and Harriet says this is because he's a complete fool and that she never liked him anyway, but I think, perhaps he has a tropical fever and his mind is wandering or perhaps he meant brown but wrote blue –

Fenwick Perhaps he has an inability to distinguish one colour from another. It is not so rare.

Harriet He cannot tell brown from blue? Don't be ridiculous.

Fenwick It's possible, Harriet, can we simply say that it's possible –

Harriet Edward's problem is that he's awash with milky sentiments lapped up from bowls of cheap poetry. In which of course the heroine's eyes are always blue –

Maria Harriet –

Harriet And I lay money on it, were you to cut his heart out, you would find it indistinguishable from tripe –

Maria Oh. How dare you! Poor Edward –

Susannah I think you've made your point, Harriet –

Maria You're jealous of me.

Harriet Of course I'm not jealous –

Susannah Girls, girls –

Maria Because he asked me to marry him and not you –

Harriet Why would I want to marry Edward? I don't want to marry anyone!

Susannah Don't be silly, Harriet, of course you do –

Harriet I do not –

Susannah Now look what you've started, Joseph!

Fenwick Me?

Susannah Your daughter doesn't want to marry. Who put that idea into her head?

Fenwick As far as I recollect, I suggested that Edward might have a problem with recognising colours. Harriet's marriage plans were not mentioned –

Susannah Not in this instance perhaps –

Roget Any chance of seeing the play?

Maria I don't want to be in her wretched play.

Roget Oh.

Harriet You may not be given to rages, Maria, but you

are most expert at sulking –

Armstrong This is as good a play as I've ever seen. Carry on, do.

Susannah Girls, girls, now come along, make up and apologise to each other, and, Harriet, stop making foolish pronouncements.

Harriet It's not foolish, I mean it, I never want to marry –

Susannah You're overexcited, dear, perhaps it's stage fright –

Harriet I am not overexcited!!!

Fenwick *rises up.*

Fenwick For God's sake, stop it, all of you!

Silence.

We have guests.

Awkward silence.

Now. When we've all calmed down, we might begin the entertainment. Perhaps you could bring everyone a glass of wine, Isobel.

Isobel Yes, sir.

She goes to pour wine.

Susannah Harriet, Maria, kiss and make up.

Harriet *and* **Maria** *kiss each other on the cheek reluctantly.*

Maria Forgive me, dearest Harriet.

Harriet Forgive me, dearest Maria.

They both look at **Susannah**.

Maria/Harriet (*together*) There.

Isobel *hands out wine.*

Susannah Excellent.

Silence as **Isobel** *puts the tray back on the table. She goes to join* **Harriet** *and* **Maria**. *They search for scripts and fiddle with them sullenly. The audience sip their wine and wait expectantly.*

Susannah Well?

Harriet All right. It won't be very good. I'm Britannia, she's Arcadia –

Susannah Yes yes yes, we know that. Get on with it.

Harriet *takes a deep breath, coughs, rustles her script.*

Harriet Well, first of all there'll just be me on stage and I'll be reading a Brief Prologue, but I haven't written that yet, and then possibly a song, which we'll all sing –

Maria Which one?

Harriet I don't know yet. One which we all know.

Susannah 'Greensleeves' perhaps.

Maria Or a hymn. I like a hymn.

Harriet It's not important at the moment –

Maria What sort of atmosphere must this song provoke?

Susannah D'you want a happy song or a sad song?

Harriet For heaven's sake I don't know yet, I wish I'd never mentioned the wretched thing.

Pause.

Maria Sorry.

Harriet Anyway, then we all come on dressed more or less like this –

Susannah I do hope you'll be doing something about Isobel's ears –

Harriet – and I will have some steam coming out of a chimney here, at least I hope so –

Maria I think perhaps you should start, Harriet.

Harriet   I'm trying to start!

Maria   Sorry, sorry.

Pause.

Harriet   So. I'm Britannia.

She clears her throat, looks at her script.

I am Britannia, spirit of our age, champion of our nation. Fair play and enterprise are my guiding lights, industry and endeavour are my saviours.

She coughs.

> I stand atop these lonely hills, from whence
> This land I view, all sage, soft gold spread out.
> The slate-grey sea, the dry stone walls I know,
> The shepherdess, her flock –

Isobel   Baaa.

Harriet   – the frisking lambs.

Maria
> But lo, on the horizon now we see –
> What can this be, what towers are rising here,
> What lights that burn so late into the night?
> That smoke that billows forth, what fires are these?

Harriet
> The future's ours, these chimneys belch out hope,
> These furnaces forge dreams as well as wealth.
> Great minds conspire to cast an Eden here
> From Iron, and steam bends nature to our will –

Maria
> The future is as new Jerusalem –

Isobel
> But not for sheep, for sheep it's looking grim.

The audience can contain their laughter no longer. **Maria** *throws down her script.*

Maria   That line ruins the entire piece, Harriet –

Isobel I told you this yesterday. I don't know why you want sheep in it anyway –

Harriet The line won't work if you say it like that –

Isobel – unless it's just an exercise in humiliation. That strikes me as a distinct possibility –

Fenwick Harriet, perhaps you should –

Harriet You're the audience, shut up –

The audience roar.

Armstrong This should transfer to Drury Lane immediately –

Harriet It wasn't my idea in the first place! You made me write it, Mama. I don't want to write plays! I don't want to write anything! Why will you insist that I am a poet? I am nothing of the sort –

Susannah Oh, come come, Harriet –

Harriet I have no talent for it whatsoever. You might wish me to be a poet, but I am not. I cannot bend words to my will, I don't want to be a poet –

Susannah We heard you the first time, dear –

Harriet I want to be a physician, like papa –

She throws down her script and storms out. Silence.

Susannah Did I hear her correctly? Did she say physician? Has she taken leave of her senses? Harriet?

She goes after her. **Maria** *follows.*

Maria Oh lord . . . Harriet, dear . . .

Fenwick *gets up.*

Fenwick Well, that's that. House full of madwomen. What about a stroll, gentlemen? Let's take a little wander down to the river –

Roget There's a blizzard out there –

Fenwick　Nonsense, Roget, you've never seen a blizzard, we call this bracing, come along –

He strides off and **Roget** *follows him.* **Isobel** *is left alone with* **Armstrong**. *She goes over to the table and begins to pull off her ears.* **Armstrong** *comes over and helps her.*

Armstrong　Oh, Isobel, Isobel, let me . . .

He nuzzles her. She is embarrassed. Pushes him away.

Isobel　Sir, this is not the place.

He looks at her, pulls her into his arms, kisses her passionately before she can resist.

Armstrong　If I give you a guinea, will you let me see you naked?

Isobel *pulls away, horrified.*

Isobel　What?

He falls on his knees.

Armstrong　A joke, a joke, and a very bad one at that –

Isobel　I am bewildered at such a jest, sir –

Armstrong　Isobel, surely you did not take me seriously? Oh God, I am mortified, why did I say that? I'm sorry. I am most truly sorry and ashamed. It's a thing I do.

Isobel　What is?

Armstrong　I make inappropriate remarks in certain situations.

Isobel　What sort of situations?

Armstrong　Those in which . . . I find myself in the grip of bewildering and powerful feelings.

He goes to the desk and sits down.

Armstrong　When my mother died I made jests at the funeral. Can you imagine? My mother whom I loved beyond anything, whom I nursed through the most wretched agony of her final illness. I don't know why I behaved as I did. I can only say that it was at odds with how I felt.

Isobel   I'm sorry for your trouble, sir.

Armstrong   Don't you see, Isobel, that I am beside myself with longing for you? I dream of you, your imprint is stamped upon my mind indelibly, I cannot help myself. Forgive me, I beg of you, and I will go, and never trouble you again.

Pause.

Isobel   There is nothing to forgive, sir.

He goes to her, kisses her hand.

Armstrong   But can you love me, Isobel?

Isobel *looks away.*

Isobel   Can you love me, sir? Surely that is more to the point.

Armstrong (*tremulously*)   I do, Isobel ... I do.

He dashes from the room. **Isobel** *hugs herself: delight, bewilderment and uncertainty battling for supremacy. Lights fade.*

Scene Two

Lights up. Main room. 1999.

Still full of packing cases etc. **Phil** *is sitting at the top of a ladder, dressed in overalls, covered in dust. He's drinking a mug of tea.*
Tom *is sorting through books, papers, old photos, general junk, and packing it into boxes.*

Phil   The whole ceiling'll have to come down.

Tom   Yeah, well, wait till we've moved out, will you?

Phil   Have you heard anything else about the body?

Tom   I've just spoken to the coroner's office. They've

done a preliminary report. Female Caucasian, between twenty and thirty, probably been there a couple of hundred years. Much longer than they thought at first. And the skeleton's incomplete.

Phil   How d'you mean?

Tom   Some of it's missing.

Phil   Poor lass. I wonder what happened to her. That's if she is a lass of course.

Tom   What d'you mean?

Phil   Well, there's some strange things go on round here. Friend of mine says they found a body up by Holy Island that's not human and it's not animal. They've never seen anything like it apparently.

Tom   Who's 'they'?

Phil   The authorities, man. They don't want to cause mass panic so they like to keep these things quiet.

Tom   Phil, they were human remains. Female human remains.

Phil   Well, they say that –

Tom   They are. I saw them. They're not Venusian or extraterrestrial in any way.

Phil   OK. Fair enough . . . D'you think she was murdered then?

Tom   The bones cut clean through, they said, with a knife or a cleaver. And crammed into a hole any old how.

Phil   In that case . . .

Phil *comes down the ladder. He goes to his tool bag and rummages around. Brings out a candle.*

Tom   What are you doing?

Phil   Emergency supplies. In case all else fails.

He sticks the candle in a piece of putty, sets it on the floor, and lights it.

Tom   What's that for?

Phil   For her soul.

Tom   Oh.

Phil   It's about time somebody did it if she's been there that long.

Tom   Oh. Right . . . Of course.

Pause.

You're a Catholic then?

Phil   Was. I still do this though.

Tom   What is it, superstition or habit?

Phil   D'you not believe in souls?

Tom   I'm not sure.

Phil   I do. I believe in reincarnation.

Tom   Is there anything you don't believe in, Phil?

Phil   Acupuncture. And Sunderland. But I still go into churches sometimes, light a candle for my mam. And I just think about her for a few minutes. I give her all my attention. I think attention's a form of prayer.

Tom   Oh. Right.

Phil *laughs.*

Phil   You think I'm mental, don't you?

He blows the candle out.

Tom   No, no, don't do that, no please, light it again –

Phil *tosses him the matches.*

Phil   You do it.

Tom *lights the candle and sets it on a packing case. They both sit on the floor and look at the flame. Silence for a while.*

Phil How's the wife's ethical crisis?

Tom Still bubbling along nicely.

Phil I had a thought.

Tom Did you?

Phil Aye.

Pause.

Tom What was it then?

Phil Bar codes.

Tom Sorry?

Phil Well, along those lines. Like you know, if they can map your genes before you're born, they'll soon be wanting a little plastic card with your DNA details on. And if it says anything dodgy, it'll be like you're credit blacked. And then imagine this, people'll say I can't have this kid because it'll never get a mortgage. I mean, that's bloody mad, that. I bet your wife hasn't thought about that, has she?

Tom I think she's starting to –

Ellen *and* **Kate** *come in, wearing outdoor clothes.*

Ellen What on earth are you doing?

Phil *gets up.*

Phil Just messing around. I'd better take this downstairs.

He goes over to his ladder, picks it up and goes out.

Ellen Did I say something?

Tom He was going anyway.

He goes back to packing.

Kate That looked very cosy. Doing a bit of male bonding, were you?

Tom We were talking about the body in the basement.

Ellen I wish you wouldn't call it that.

Kate   She probably wasn't murdered. She was dissected. That's why some of her's missing.

Tom   What makes you think this?

Kate   I remember years ago, they had to dig up an old cemetery near us, to widen the road. And when they came to move the coffins, lots of the really old ones were empty. The bodies had been snatched. Probably by medical students, before the Anatomy Act, which was about eighteen thirtysomething.

Ellen   So why then bury her in our garden?

Kate   I don't know. Nearest place maybe. It'd be a bit risky trying to put her back in her grave. Risky enough getting her out in the first place.

Ellen   There you are, Tom. Not a murder victim at all. Just the equivalent of leaving your body for medical research. Feel better now?

He stares into the candle flame, and blows it out. Blackout. They leave.

Roget *and* **Armstrong** *enter, in outdoor clothes, carrying racquets. The two men blow on their hands, stamp to keep warm.* **Roget** *takes a shuttlecock from his pocket and they begin to play.*

Armstrong   You should have been there. A growth the size of a potato.

Roget   Jersey or King Edward?

Armstrong   Bigger in fact. As big as my fist. In the upper abdominal cavity. Smaller ones in the lungs. The smell was abominable, of course.

Roget   Where did you get him from?

Armstrong   Who?

Roget   The unfortunate stinking corpse.

Armstrong   I've no idea. Farleigh saw to it.

Roget   Ah.

Armstrong   Ah what?

Roget   Was it still in its grave clothes by any chance?

Armstrong   It was stark naked on a slab. I don't know why you're playing holier than thou.

He stretches for a shot and misses, crashing his racquet down on the table.

Damn.

Roget   Mind the table!

He goes over and rubs at it with his coat sleeve. **Armstrong** *picks up the shuttlecock and bats it back to* **Roget.**

Roget   The whole thing sticks in my craw ever since two students in Edinburgh acquired for us a lovely fresh corpse which turned out to be our tutor's grandfather. The poor man clean fainted away when he pulled back the sheet.

Armstrong   What difference does it make if they're dead? The dead are just meat. But meat that tells a story. Every time I slice open a body, I feel as if I'm discovering America.

Roget   I do see the relatives' point. If you believe in bodily resurrection, the minimum requirement is a body.

Armstrong   I'd happily allow you to slice mine into porterhouse steaks, as long as I was definitively dead.

Roget   When's Farleigh's next demonstration?

Armstrong   Depends on the supply. D'you want to come?

Roget   I'm torn. I'm fascinated by the thing itself but slightly uneasy at the methods used to procure the bodies.

Armstrong   We've got our eye on an undersized fellow, about three foot tall. He's not at all well. He'll not see out the winter.

Roget   You seek out potential cadavers before they're even dead?

He catches the shuttlecock and stops playing.

Good God, man, that's appalling.

Armstrong   Needs must. We can have any number of average, everyday corpses. They're two a penny. Literally, at this time of year, when people are dropping like flies. But an unusual specimen must be ordered in advance. I thought you knew that?

Roget   I suppose I didn't think about it. I didn't ask where they came from, I assumed . . .

Armstrong   What? That they climbed on to the dissecting table of their own accord?

Roget   No no no, of course not, I just . . . well, I suppose I chose not to wonder.

He bats the shuttlecock to **Armstrong**.

Armstrong   You didn't want to sully yourself with thoughts of such vile trade. You're a romantic, Roget –

Roget   I think more precisely, I am a man of delicate sensibilities –

Armstrong   Useless, not to say dangerous, qualities in a man of science.

Roget   D'you never have qualms? D'you exist solely in the burning fires of certainty?

Armstrong   Digging up corpses is necessary if we're to totter out of the Dark Ages. You can dissect a stolen body with moral qualms or with none at all and it won't make a blind bit of difference to what you discover. Discovery is neutral. Ethics should be left to philosophers and priests. I've never had a moral qualm in my life, and it would be death to science if I did. That's why I'll be remembered as a great physician, Roget, and you'll be forgotten as a man who made lists.

Roget *passes him a drop shot which he fails to anticipate and misses.*

Armstrong   Bastard.

Fenwick *appears. They stop playing, guiltily.*

Roget   Sir – we were just, er –

Armstrong   It was very cold outside, sir.

Fenwick   Useless girls, both of you. Anyway. Supper's about to be served.

They go with him.

Lights down. **Maria** *reads a letter over the scene change.*

Maria   'Dear Edward, You are right, England is cold and bleak, and so, I might add is my heart. Either distance has dimmed your perception of me, or you never looked properly at me from the start. Imagine my eyes again, Edward. Now write and tell me what colour they appear in your imagination. Your early letters were so full of longing for me and for home, but now I sense a reluctance to return which cannot entirely be explained by the prevailing weather conditions. I hear, via a Mr Roger Thornton, who has recently returned from Lucknow, that a certain Miss Cholmondely has stayed in India rather longer than expected. Could this be the same musical creature you mention in your letters? She who sinks into a dead faint when confronted by native antiquities? Her eyes, I gather, are a quite startling blue. I note that when you think of England now you remember dead boys frozen in the top meadow. Hitherto you imagined soft sunlight and balmy breezes and gentle Englishmen full of decorum and equanimity. I now realise that your vision of England was as flawed as your recollection of my eyes. Yes, it is true that here we may freeze to death in winter. Indeed our summers are mild. But temperate we are not. Need I remind you that we have had bloody riots here for at least six months, and that my father, the finest Englishman I know, has never been anything less than passionate. As you know, Edward, I have long been regarded as the mild, perhaps even silly half of the heavenly twins, very much in Harriet's poetic shadow. That, presumably, is what attracted you to me in the first place. (But Miss Cholmondely is clearly the better swooner.) I find now, however, that anger has provoked my intellect like a spark igniting a long-dormant volcano. I await your reply with interest. Sincerely, Maria Fenwick.'

Scene Three

Lights up on a long table, lit with candelabra.

Fenwick, Susannah, Maria, Roget *and* **Armstrong** *seated. Supper is over, and they are eating fruit, drinking.* **Isobel** *is clearing away plates and glasses. Everyone is a little the worse for wear, particularly* **Susannah**.

Fenwick   When you've finished, Isobel, you may come and join us if you wish.

Susannah   You prefer to talk to the servants than to me, Joseph.

Fenwick   Don't be ridiculous, Susannah.

Susannah   I am not being ridiculous. It's patronising to ask the girl to fetch and carry on the one hand and join us for elevating conversation on the other.

She pours herself more wine. Hands **Isobel** *the empty bottle.*

Bring up another bottle please, Isobel.

Isobel   Yes, madam.

She goes out with tray of crockery etc. as **Harriet** *comes in wearing her bonnet with the chimney. The chimney is now belching puffs of steam.*

Harriet   Papa, Mama! Here you are. Look! I told you I would get it to work.

They all look. Murmurs of delight.

Fenwick   Oh, well done, Harriet –

Roget   I say! Look at that!

Susannah   Look at what? What am I supposed to be looking at?

Maria   Her bonnet, Mama!

Susannah   What about it?

Armstrong   The steam, madam, the steam –

Susannah   Good God –

The steam stops puffing.

Harriet   Oh. It's stopped –

Roget   Nevertheless, Harriet, a remarkable achievement –

Harriet   Papa? Are you proud of me?

Fenwick   Impressed beyond words. It was almost worth sitting through that dreadful play, if this is one of the serendipitous results –

Susannah   But when would you wear such a thing, dear?

Harriet   That's not the point, Mama, the point is that through experiment I have made a discovery –

Susannah   But a singularly useless one –

Fenwick   Susannah, shut up. Harriet, my dear, sit down and have some wine. I'm delighted and impressed.

Harriet *sits down, glowing.*

Susannah   Mark the contemptuous way my husband speaks to me, gentlemen –

Fenwick   Susannah, that's enough –

Susannah   Tell me, Mr Roget, do you think my husband a saint?

Roget   I'm sorry?

Susannah   St Joseph of Newcastle upon Tyne. How would that suit him?

Roget   I think him a exemplary man, a great scientist and fine physician. However, sainthood would seem to be stretching a point.

Susannah   But you think him a man of great principle, with a finely tuned conscience, considerate to servants, indulgent to his family, yes?

Roget   Well ... on balance, I would say so, yes.

Susannah   Then allow me to tell you how profoundly wrong you are.

Fenwick   Susannah –

Susannah   Don't worry, I'm not about to reveal any scandal. Oh, gentlemen, if only he were scandalous, but I'm afraid he's much too dull for that. What he is, is indifferent. To me. And what wife can stand that?

Armstrong   I wonder if we should perhaps retire to the drawing-room, Roget –

He begins to get up.

Susannah   Sit down!

Armstrong   Of course.

He sits down again abruptly.

Harriet   May Maria and I be excused, Papa?

Susannah   No!

Silence.

Fenwick   Susannah –

Susannah   And because you all admire him, that makes you indifferent too! It is intolerable. In my own house to be constantly ignored, to be held in no account –

Roget   Madam, I assure you that this is not the case, please. I beg of you –

Susannah   And if I am a little drunk, what of it, you too would be drunk if you had to bear what I must bear –

Fenwick   Susannah, no one is indifferent to you –

Susannah   Liar!

Isobel *returns with more wine.* **Susannah** *takes it from her, pours herself more.*

Susannah   You don't love me.

Awkward silence. **Isobel** *hovers.*

Fenwick   What's this nonsense now?

Maria   Mama, we all love you. Indeed we do.

Susannah   The most respected man in the region, the most philanthropic, whose learning is universally admired, has no time for his own wife.

Armstrong   I'm sure you are grossly mistaken –

Susannah   He has turned me into a joke. I could play patience stark naked and he'd not notice.

Roget   Madam –

Susannah   And neither would you.

Harriet   Mama, please!

Susannah   I even embarrass my own children. I sit in a corner and chirrup away like a canary. Why don't you get a cage for me and a nice bit of cuttlefish. In fact, when we had a canary, he paid more attention to it than to me, he thought it intriguing and fascinating, all the things he once felt about me –

Fenwick   You have had a little too much wine, Susannah –

Susannah   I am shut out from everything you do. You think me a fool!

Fenwick   Of course I don't think you a fool –

Susannah   Because I care more for Shakespeare than for Newton.

Fenwick They are not in competition, Susannah. One does not cancel out the other. They form a complementarity, not a state of siege.

Susannah I admit I had little education when I married him, but that was no fault of mine. I painted, read poetry and plays, a little Greek of course, but obviously that counts for nothing.

Roget On the contrary, it sounds quite admirable.

Susannah *gets up and thumps her breast theatrically.*

Susannah I am an artist, gentlemen! I have a soul!

Silence.

Maria Mama, do stop it.

Susannah I am full of feeling and passion and I am wedded to a dried cod.

She sits down again, in tears.

Isobel Um. Will that be all, sir?

Fenwick Of course, Isobel, off you go.

He gets up.

Please don't feel you must stay, gentlemen. My wife is a little overwrought –

Susannah Overwrought!

Fenwick Harriet, Maria, go with the gentlemen into the drawing-room, will you?

Harriet/Maria (*together*) Yes, Papa.

They get up.

Roget Madam.

Armstrong Madam.

They get up to leave.

Susannah That's right, go. Leave me to fend for myself –

Roget *and* **Armstrong** *hesitate.*

Fenwick We'll join you presently, gentlemen.

They all go out. Silence. **Susannah** *continues to cry.*

Fenwick Susannah –

Susannah I'm sorry. I'm sorry, Joseph.

Fenwick So you should be.

Susannah Don't speak to me like a child! I am not a wayward infant to be scolded indulgently, I am your wife! Listen to me when I talk to you, take notice of what I say. Do not dismiss it as precocious whimsy! I want you to take me seriously, do you understand, Joseph?

Fenwick *is flustered.*

Fenwick I'm very . . . I'm sorry, Susannah –

Susannah So you should be.

Fenwick Very well, now we're all square.

Susannah Stop it! Stop patronising me. It's like a twitch, Joseph, you do it without thinking.

Pause.

Fenwick I don't know what you want me to say, Susannah.

Susannah When you married me, Joseph, you thought me beautiful.

Fenwick I still think that.

Susannah But you never mentioned any other requirements. The fact that I knew nothing of politics or science seemed a matter of supreme indifference to you, in fact you found my ignorance delightful, charming even.

Fenwick I didn't know it was ignorance. I thought it an affectation of your sex and class.

Susannah You loved me, Joseph, you pursued me with such tenderness, such dogged devotion, how could I not love you in return? Because the choice was not mine, d'you understand? I never had the freedom to choose as you did –

Fenwick I didn't force you to marry me, Susannah –

Susannah I was a passive thing, waiting to be filled up with love and ooze it out in return. That is what young women do, Joseph, they wait to be loved, they wait for a man to bestow his mysterious gift upon them. I loved you because you loved me. That was my criterion. What else did I have to go on? What else did I know? You caused this love in me! You planted it in me and then you abandoned it!

Fenwick I haven't abandoned you, Susannah.

Susannah But that is what it feels like, Joseph. I am lonely. It is a lonely thing to be married to you.

Pause.

Fenwick It seems I've been remiss in my affection, and I am most profoundly sorry. Perhaps I've been too bound up with my work –

Susannah Bound up? You have given your entire life over to it! Oh, certainly you have feelings, indeed you do, you are stuffed to bursting point with feelings about this injustice here, that cruelty there. You have feelings for every passing stray but none whatsoever for me. I've watched you weep bitter tears, I've watched you tear your hair at the misfortunes of utter strangers, whilst my most palpable misery goes sublimely unacknowledged –

Fenwick It was never my intention to make you unhappy, Susannah –

Susannah How could you love me so much then and so little now? Am I not the same person? Perhaps the woman you professed such tenderness towards then was an invention, a construct of your imagination –

Fenwick   I did love you, Susannah –

Susannah   Did? What good is did to me?

Fenwick   Do, I do love you, but perhaps we interpret the word in different ways. You talk of tenderness when you talk of love, you talk of dogged devotion, you make it all sweet nothings and new hair ribbons –

Susannah   I dispute the last, but for the rest, what else is love but tender devotion –

Fenwick   I was in thrall to you, Susannah. Sick, weak with longing at the merest hint of your presence. I couldn't sleep for thinking of the web of veins that traced the inside of your arms. I dreamt of the scent of your neck, the soft, suckable lobe of your ear. I wanted to crush your mouth against mine, I wanted to run my tongue down the cleft your breasts –

Susannah   Joseph, please, this is bedroom talk –

Fenwick   – I wanted to lose myself inside you. Your beauty possessed me, it made my blood dance. I could watch the pulse flickering in your wrist and feel sick with desire. But because you were beautiful I imagined you to be wise, and yes I know now, as I knew then, that one has nothing to do with the other. I asked myself even then, do I love her because she is beautiful or is she beautiful because I love her. I couldn't answer and I didn't care. Passion distorts, it makes things seem what they are not. Because you had the face of the Madonna, I imbued you with her qualities. You had not conversation then, and I told myself that still waters run deep. Your looks of blank incomprehension I read as philosophical musing. When I talked of politics or science, and your face betrayed no expression whatsoever, I saw it as profound spiritual calm, a stillness which put my passion to shame, I saw in you a wisdom which I could never hope to attain. The less you said the easier it was to invent you. You could have sat at my side and warbled in Japanese and I would have hung on to your every word. I dreamt of your flesh, I wanted to lick your eyes, I wanted to leave children inside you . . .

Pause.

Susannah Joseph, if you bear any vestige of that love for me, you must make it manifest. You must talk to me in a language which does not exclude me. Do not shut me out. Do not humiliate me in front of your friends, but include me, ask my advice, my opinion. I know I behave ridiculously, don't imagine I am unaware of it. I loathe the role I have taken on, but you forced me to it, d'you understand? It's the only part you have left open to me and I have played it to the hilt. You talk always of equality. Why don't you practice it? I want to be your equal, not a fawning, yapping lap dog –

Isobel *appears. Screaming and shouting offstage.*

Isobel I'm sorry, sir, madam . . .

Harriet *and* **Maria** *come hurtling in, screaming at each other and wrestling each other to the ground.*

Maria Take that back! Take it back!

Harriet Never! Argh . . . get off me, get off – Papa, Papa –

Susannah Girls, girls, what on earth –

Harriet *manages to disentangle herself slightly.*

Harriet Edward is a fickle fool, Maria, anyone could have told you that, the whole world knew of his passion for Miss Cholmondely apart from you –

Maria *goes for her again.*

Maria How dare you, how dare you –

Fenwick Harriet, Maria!

They ignore him and continue fighting.

Maria I hate you, I hate you –

Fenwick *grabs* **Maria** *and* **Susannah** *drags off the struggling* **Harriet**.

Susannah   Stop fighting immediately!

Harriet   Stop it, stop it, get off me –

She tries to kick **Susannah**.

Fenwick   Harriet, for once in your life, listen to your mother and do as she says –

Harriet *is so stunned she shuts up. Both girls are carted offstage.* **Maria** *bawling 'I hate her! I hate her!'*

Isobel *begins to clear away the rest of the debris from the table.* **Armstrong** *comes in, unnoticed. He tiptoes up behind her, puts his arms around her waist. She gasps, and he puts his hand over her mouth, turns her round towards himself and kisses her passionately. He pushes her over the table.*

Armstrong   Isobel . . . I adore you, Isobel . . . I adore you . . .

He kisses her again.

I want you to take this. It belonged to my mother.

He hands her something wrapped in a piece of silk.

Just tell me, I just want to know, that's all . . . Just tell me that you might be able to love me.

Pause. **Isobel** *clutches the gift and speaks in a shy whisper.*

Isobel   I believe I might, sir . . .

She kisses him. He pushes her on to the table, kisses her again. Suddenly **Roget** *appears.*

Roget   Armstrong? What in God's name d'you think you're doing?

The two spring apart. **Isobel** *pulls herself together and slithers off the table.*

Isobel   Excuse me, sir, excuse me –

She dashes out. **Armstrong** *straightens his clothes and pours himself a drink.*

Armstrong You shouldn't burst in on people like that.

Roget What were you doing?

Armstrong I was kissing her passionately. What did it look like?

Roget How could you?

Armstrong It was quite easy actually, she didn't object in the least. Why should she?

Roget You can't play with her like this.

Armstrong Oh, I think perhaps jealousy rears its ugly head.

Roget It's nothing of the sort, I just can't bear to see the girl led by the nose.

Armstrong She knows the state of play, she's not stupid.

Roget Far from it, but she's ignorant when it comes to these particular matters, and you know it.

Armstrong I enjoy her company.

Roget So do I.

Armstrong I think you might find she enjoys my company rather more extravagantly than she does yours. I'm sorry, but there it is. What can I do about it?

Roget What do you want from her?

Armstrong *laughs.*

Armstrong I love her, it's as simple as that.

Roget So you love her. But not enough, I presume, to marry her.

Armstrong Marriage is a different thing entirely. I'll probably marry a woman with a face like a horse but a great deal of money in the bank. I don't expect it will have anything much to do with love.

Roget   What is it that you particularly love about Isobel?

Isobel *appears in the doorway. Neither notice her. She stays in the shadows and listens.*

Armstrong   Oh, this and that. Who can say really? Love's such an indefinable thing, isn't it, I mean . . .

He begins to giggle.

Oh, for God's sake, Roget, I can't keep this up another minute, of course I don't bloody love her.

Roget   I knew you didn't.

Armstrong   I almost had you convinced though, didn't I?

Roget   Not for a moment actually.

Armstrong   'Oh Isobel, Isobel I adore you!'

He giggles.

God, I don't know how I managed it. She really is very hard work.

Roget   So why in hell's name are you doing it to her?

Armstrong   It's all in a good cause, I assure you.

Roget   What cause?

Armstrong   There's nothing sinister in it, honestly, it's all rather innocent actually. I don't know why you never thought of it yourself. So. I tell her I love her and so forth, right?

Roget   Yes . . .

Armstrong   I flatter her, look suitably love struck when she comes into a room, I call her beautiful –

Roget   But why? –

Armstrong   And eventually I get her into the sack.

Roget   That would seem to be a logical, if cynical progression. It's not in itself an explanation.

Armstrong   Oh, for God's sake, man, I get her in the sack which means she takes off her clothes –

Roget   Not necessarily –

Armstrong   I make sure she takes them off, that's the whole point because then I get to examine her beautiful back in all its delicious, twisted glory, and frankly that's all I'm interested in. D'you know the first time I saw it I got an erection?

Roget   You find it arousing?

Armstrong   In the same way that I find electricity exciting, or the isolation of oxygen, or the dissection of a human heart.

Roget *stares at him.*

Armstrong   I told you it was all in a good cause, didn't I? I mean, obviously she's not the sort to just take her clothes off and let me have a look for a few bob, I spotted the Presbyterian bent right away. In fact I almost scuppered my chances at one point, before I'd got the full measure of her. I had to make up some awful rubbish about my mother being dead, which of course she isn't. So unfortunately we have to go the long route. Farleigh showed us a similar torso once but it was much milder. Extraordinary malformation of the upper vertebrae, with resultant distortion of the rib cage. And hers, you see, is much more severe, much more interesting, I mean it's exquisite, it's almost a poem –

Isobel *runs off, stifling a cry.* **Roget** *turns round.*

Roget   What was that?

Armstrong   What? Nothing.

Roget *looks at him.*

Roget   Can I say something?

Armstrong *grins.*

Armstrong   Go ahead.

Roget   You are amoral, corrupt and depraved. You are cruel, heartless, mean spirited, barbarous. You are treacherous, despicable, and vilely contemptible. You are a low-down seducer. You're a cunt, Armstrong. A complete and utter cunt.

He goes out. **Armstrong** *shrugs, genuinely baffled at this response.*

Armstrong   Why? What have I done?

Lights fade. He goes out. Enter **Maria** *who reads a letter over scene change.*

Maria   'Dear Edward, Thank you for your sloppily written missive. I note that you and Miss Cholmondely have indeed become "firm friends" and I am not at all sorry that you will no longer be returning to England. You have recently been the source of great animosity between my dear sister and myself, for which rupture I blame you entirely. Our quarrel resulted, I am sorry to say, in no small degree of violence. I long for something similar, but more extreme, to light upon yourself, and only wish I were able to deliver the blows myself. Please do not write to me again. Maria Fenwick.'

Scene Four

1999. Lights up on same room as before, one tea chest left. The table bears the remnants of a meal, as in the previous scene. **Tom** *is sitting at the head of the table, in what was previously* **Susannah**'s *place.* **Ellen** *is next to him.*

Tom   So you're taking the job. I suppose I should say congratulations.

He raises his glass.

Mind you, I don't know why you even pretended to consider your options. You were never really going to turn it down, were you?

Ellen   I might have done. I could have stayed where I

am, and kept my hands clean. I could have avoided filthy commercialism and struggled along on bits of funding from now till doomsday. I did consider it actually. But this is too exciting. I can't resist it, basically. It wasn't an intellectual decision. It was my heart. I felt it beat faster when I thought of the all the possibilities.

Tom Apparently the heart is involved in the choices we make. Literally. It's not just a pump. That's a scientific fact.

Ellen According to who?

Tom I read it somewhere. It's the main motor of the body. It's what drives us, it's what defines us. You're not just your brain. Apparently, if you give someone a new heart, they quite often take on some of the characteristics of the donor –

Ellen Have you been talking to Phil?

Tom The heart retains information, they don't understand how, yet, but everything's connected one way or another, nothing exists in isolation. When you feel grief, your heart hurts. When you feel love, it's your heart that hurts, not your brain. You took this job because your heart told you to.

Ellen You make it sound poetic.

Tom Isn't it?

Ellen Science is supposed to be cold and considered and rational.

Tom But it's not, is it?

Ellen In practice, it is. But I suppose my urge to pursue it is a passion, it's intense, the same as yours for George Eliot or John Webster. Actually, it's more than that. It's sexy. It makes me fizz inside. To me it's a form of rapture. You're right. To me, an exquisitely balanced formula is a poem.

Tom So we're not that much different after all. Art and science are part of the same thing. Like waves and particles. You need both to define the whole.

Ellen Maybe. But you stirred up questions in me and I blamed you for it. I'd never felt unconfident before. Not about work anyway. The bottom line is: I don't think science is value free, I don't think it's morally neutral. Kate does, but I don't –

Kate *comes in with two more bottles of wine.*

Kate What do I do?

Tom You're unscrupulous, ambitious, and you'd dissect your own mother if you thought it might give you the answer to something.

Kate Yeah, I probably would. But only if she was dead already.

Tom So where would you draw the line?

Kate Well, I wouldn't kill. I wouldn't murder. But apart from that . . . white or red?

Tom Red, please. But would you have worked on developing the atomic bomb, say –

Ellen She's a geneticist, Tom.

Tom I know, but the ramifications are similar –

Ellen You can't not pursue something. You can't say the road might have complications so I won't go down it. Once you know something, you can't unknow it –

Kate The thing is, Tom, I can't make you see the world the way that I do. For me it's all potential, it's all possibility, everything's there to be unravelled and decoded. We're discovering things so fast now, we're falling over our feet. It's like for me everything is total possibility and for you everything is total remembrance.

Tom Well, I don't know, shall I just cut my throat now? Why wait?

Kate I want to eat up the world, I want to tear it apart and see what it's made of. And you're just conscious of this weight all the time, of the past bearing down on you –

Tom   The past's always with us –

Kate   There's nothing wrong with Milton, there's nothing wrong with Shakespeare –

Tom   I'm glad we've sorted that out then –

Kate   But it's history, and I'm hooked on the future.

Tom   Don't you think there is something to be said for acknowledging the weight of history?

Kate   Yes, but –

Tom   No you don't, you don't even know what history is –

Kate   Oh please –

Tom   You don't respect ambiguities –

Kate   What on earth does that mean?

Tom   You bandy these words about, like manic depression and schizophrenia, and you don't even know what they mean. Schizophrenia is just a label, it's not a finite quantifiable thing –

Kate   Schizophrenia can cause untold misery –

Tom   Not necessarily, and not that you care anyway, I mean, that's not why you do it, is it –

Kate   No, why should it be –

Ellen   Tom, we've been through this –

Tom   James Joyce probably had a schizophrenia gene, his daughter certainly did. It's a continuum, at one end you get poetry and at the other confusion, you can't just swat it like a fly. You don't understand the world at all, only your tidy version of it, you do all your experiments in a vacuum –

Kate   Tom, that's a very nice romantic idea, but it's not true, you're hopeless, you're a dinosaur –

Tom   Yeah, well, we look around, us dinosaurs, and we know we're old and tired, a bit cynical, a bit ironic, but we know the score, we can see the arc of things. We've seen things come and go. And one of the things we know is that the Messiah's not coming. We know that much.

She laughs and hands him his wine.

Kate   How d'you know? How come you're so certain?

Tom   Oh, for goodness sake –

Kate   I'm telling you, Tom, we don't know anything, but it's out there now, within our grasp. Does that not blow your mind?

Tom   Not in the way you'd like it to –

Phil *appears.*

Phil   Right, I'm off then, have a good New Year.

Ellen   Phil, stay, have a drink before you go –

Tom   Have one to see in the new century, stop us arguing, for God's sake –

Phil   Oh, go on then, a quick one –

Kate *hands him a glass of wine. They all drink.*

All   Cheers –

Phil   In twenty-four hours it'll be the twenty-first century then. It doesn't feel like it, does it?

Tom   How's it supposed to feel?

Phil   I don't know. Futuristic. Not like this. It feels a bit old-fashioned, like. You know, you think it's going to be robots and everything shiny-white and new and clean. That's what it's like in the films. The future. But it's just the same old shite really, isn't it?

He looks at his watch.

I'd better go. I've got to take my daughter to the hospital.

He downs his drink.

Thanks a lot then. Have a good New Year.

They get up and raise their glasses.

All   Happy New Year!

He goes out. The others are frozen, glasses aloft, as **Isobel** *comes in with paper and pencil and the silk-wrapped gift from* **Armstrong**. *She opens it: a gold chain. She holds it up to the light and puts it around her neck. She reads through a letter she has just written.*

Isobel   'Loving words as I do, I now find my vocabulary insufficient to describe my anguish. How may I explain to you my fall from contentment to despair? I was never a loved thing; it was not a condition I had ever known. Recently, and most fleetingly, I discovered the rapture of that state. Now I know it to have been a fiction. My life stretches before me, and it is now a bitter road. All pleasure's pale now that I have felt love and may never feel it again. You will say that it was not a real love, and I would agree. It was a lie and it was moonshine, but how happy I was to bathe in its watery glow. Now my mouth is full of ashes. He caused dreams in me where none had thrived before, and I am without hope or consolation. Isobel Bridie'

Isobel *folds the letter. Blackout.*

Scene Five

Lights up. **Isobel** *is hanging from a rope in the middle of the stage, the chair overturned beneath her dangling feet.*

Maria *comes on. She screams.* **Armstrong** *comes running on.*

Armstrong   Oh my God, oh my God –

He runs to the body, climbs on the chair, tries to get her down. **Maria** *is frozen with horror.*

Armstrong   Help me, help me, Maria, for God's sake –

She helps him and together they get **Isobel** *down.*

Maria   Oh, Isobel, Isobel, I don't understand –

She feels for a pulse. **Armstrong** *puts his ear to* **Isobel***'s chest.*

I can feel a pulse, it's weak but it's there –

Armstrong *takes off his coat and places it under* **Isobel***'s head.*

Armstrong   Fetch help, Maria, find your father, anyone –

Maria   They're out walking –

Armstrong   Well, find them!

She goes. **Armstrong** *feels the side of* **Isobel***'s neck for a pulse.*

Armstrong   Isobel? Can you hear me?

There's no response. He hesitates. Then puts his hands over her nose and mouth, presses down. Her heels flutter almost imperceptibly. In a second it is over. He feels her pulse again. He gets up, shakily and notices that the letter lying underneath the chair. He picks it up, unfold its it. Reads.

'Loving words as I do . . .'

He reads to the end, then crumples the paper and puts it in his pocket. **Fenwick**, **Roget**, **Harriet**, **Maria** *and* **Susannah** *come in.*

Armstrong   She's gone. I couldn't save her.

Fenwick *and* **Roget** *go to her. The three women hold on to each other in horror.*

Fenwick   Why? Why did she do this?

Susannah   She left no note, no explanation?

Armstrong   It seems not.

Fenwick   Isobel, did we not care for you enough? Were we harsh? What did we do?

Susannah *goes to her.*

Susannah   Oh, her poor neck.

She takes her hand.

Are you sure she's dead, Joseph?

Fenwick Gone. Snuffed out.

He picks her up in his arms. Tears run down his face.

I'll take her to her room. She should lie on a soft bed not a cold floor. Come with me.

He goes out. The women follow. **Roget** *and* **Armstrong** *are left. Silence.*

Armstrong Why did you tell her, you stupid fool?

Roget I didn't. She was at the door. She heard what you said about her.

Pause.

Armstrong Well, how was I to know? It's not my fault, I didn't know she was . . .

Roget What?

Armstrong Unstable. I didn't know. Don't say anything, eh?

Silence.

I mean, we don't know for a fact that it was me who drove her to it, do we? It could have been anything.

Roget Of course it was you.

Armstrong Where's the evidence?

Roget You disgust me.

Armstrong I never wished her dead.

Roget Much more convenient that she is. I expect she won't be in her grave five minutes before Farleigh has her dug up.

Armstrong *giggles nervously.*

Armstrong Oh, well. Waste not want not . . .

Roget *walks over to him and punches him hard in the stomach. He doubles over in agony as* **Roget** *walks out. He staggers out after him as* **Tom** *and* **Ellen** *come in. They look round the empty room.*

Ellen We could still pull out. Contracts aren't signed yet.

Tom No. Let's sell up and get out. Let's start again.

Ellen Are you sure?

Tom Yes. It's just a house. I think they should knock it down actually.

Ellen What?

Tom It's had its day. It's worn out. You can't keep adapting this bit and converting that bit. Knock it down and build something new. Something wonderful. There was a medieval almshouse on the site before they built this place and they knocked that down with confidence. Kate thinks I worship the past but I don't. I just liked this house, but fuck it, I want to be free of it now. I'm sick of being shackled to dry rot and deathwatch beetles. We'll start again. It could be exciting even.

Ellen You'll get another job.

Tom I doubt it. I'm going to sail into the twenty-first century as a middle-aged redundant man supported by a younger sexier wife who works at the cutting edge of technology. Maybe there's a sort of poetic justice to it.

Ellen You're only redundant as an English lecturer. You're not redundant as as human being.

Tom I keep thinking about the dead girl, do you? No upper vertebrae. Missing ribs. That's the bit I don't understand.

Ellen I don't suppose we ever will.

Tom No.

Pause.

This time next year, this room will be full of Scandinavian

businessmen leaping out of saunas and drinking schnapps and shouting skol.

Ellen   I bet it's not. They'll probably run out of money by June and the place'll be left abandoned, halfway between a bunker and a shopping centre. This time next year there'll be pigeons in here and security fences outside. And in five years' time they'll pull it down. And build a car park.

Tom   And no one will remember the dead girl in the kitchen garden except us.

Ellen   I think I'll be glad to leave now.

Tom   Let's go and put the champagne in the fridge.

They go out as the lights dim. Music, distant sounds of what could be celebrations, or could be riots. Chandelier descends, **Roget** *and* **Armstrong** *carry on* **Isobel***'s open coffin.* **Harriet** *and* **Maria** *follow them with tall flickering candles. The coffin is placed gently on the table. They gather round to look at her.*

Harriet   Poor Isobel.

Roget   She looks almost beautiful. Pale as wax. One might hardly notice her poor back. It seems, now, the least significant thing about her.

Armstrong   (*gazing at her, fascinated*)   She is exquisite. She makes a beautiful corpse.

They look at him.

As Roget said . . . So pale and waxen.

Maria   What time is it?

Harriet   It must be almost midnight.

Fenwick *and* **Susannah** *come in. They go to the coffin.* **Fenwick** *kisses* **Isobel***'s forehead,* **Susannah** *strokes her hair.*

Fenwick   So this is how we're seeing out the century. Not the way we'd imagined it, not with a flurry of trumpets and beacons blazing. I thought it would be a golden night, full of hope and anticipation, and instead, this. Groping blindly over the border in a fog of bewilderment. The future looks less benign now, Isobel. We're a little more frightened than we were.

He kisses her again. **Susannah** *strokes her hair.*

Susannah   I don't understand . . . I don't understand . . .

Fenwick   Goodbye, Isobel . . .

The lighting changes as they gather round the coffin, to the chiaroscuro effects of the very first montage. Their positions and attitudes once again suggest the painting, but this time **Isobel**, *in her coffin, has taken the place of the bird in the air pump. The rioting continues from outside.* **Fenwick** *looks at his pocket watch.*

Susannah   Are they rioting or celebrating out there?

Fenwick   It's hard to tell . . .

He lifts his right arm for silence as the bells ring out the chimes of midnight.

Fenwick   Here's to whatever lies ahead . . . here's to uncharted lands . . . here's to a future we dream about but cannot know . . . here's to the new century.

Music. Hold on montage. Lights fade.

Methuen Drama Student Editions

Jean Anouilh *Antigone* • John Arden *Serjeant Musgrave's Dance*
Alan Ayckbourn *Confusions* • Aphra Behn *The Rover* • Edward Bond
Lear • *Saved* • Bertolt Brecht *The Caucasian Chalk Circle* • *Fear and
Misery in the Third Reich* • *The Good Person of Szechwan* • *Life of Galileo* •
Mother Courage and her Children • *The Resistible Rise of Arturo Ui* • *The
Threepenny Opera* • Anton Chekhov *The Cherry Orchard* • *The Seagull* •
Three Sisters • *Uncle Vanya* • Caryl Churchill *Serious Money* • *Top Girls*
• Shelagh Delaney *A Taste of Honey* • Euripides *Elektra* • *Medea*•
Dario Fo *Accidental Death of an Anarchist* • Michael Frayn *Copenhagen*
• John Galsworthy *Strife* • Nikolai Gogol *The Government Inspector* •
Robert Holman *Across Oka* • Henrik Ibsen *A Doll's House* • *Ghosts*•
Hedda Gabler • Charlotte Keatley *My Mother Said I Never Should* •
Bernard Kops *Dreams of Anne Frank* • Federico García Lorca *Blood
Wedding* • *Doña Rosita the Spinster* (bilingual edition) •*The House of
Bernarda Alba* • (bilingual edition) • *Yerma* (bilingual edition) • David
Mamet *Glengarry Glen Ross* • *Oleanna* • Patrick Marber *Closer* • John
Marston *Malcontent* • Martin McDonagh *The Lieutenant of Inishmore* •
Joe Orton *Loot* • Luigi Pirandello *Six Characters in Search of an Author*
• Mark Ravenhill *Shopping and F***ing* • Willy Russell *Blood Brothers*
• *Educating Rita* • Sophocles *Antigone* • *Oedipus the King* • Wole
Soyinka *Death and the King's Horseman* • Shelagh Stephenson *The
Memory of Water* • August Strindberg *Miss Julie* • J. M. Synge *The
Playboy of the Western World* • Theatre Workshop *Oh What a Lovely
War* Timberlake Wertenbaker *Our Country's Good* • Arnold Wesker
The Merchant • Oscar Wilde *The Importance of Being Earnest* •
Tennessee Williams *A Streetcar Named Desire* • *The Glass Menagerie*

Methuen Drama Modern Plays

include work by

Edward Albee	Howard Korder
Jean Anouilh	Robert Lepage
John Arden	Doug Lucie
Margaretta D'Arcy	Martin McDonagh
Peter Barnes	John McGrath
Sebastian Barry	Terrence McNally
Brendan Behan	David Mamet
Dermot Bolger	Patrick Marber
Edward Bond	Arthur Miller
Bertolt Brecht	Mtwa, Ngema & Simon
Howard Brenton	Tom Murphy
Anthony Burgess	Phyllis Nagy
Simon Burke	Peter Nichols
Jim Cartwright	Sean O'Brien
Caryl Churchill	Joseph O'Connor
Complicite	Joe Orton
Noël Coward	Louise Page
Lucinda Coxon	Joe Penhall
Sarah Daniels	Luigi Pirandello
Nick Darke	Stephen Poliakoff
Nick Dear	Franca Rame
Shelagh Delaney	Mark Ravenhill
David Edgar	Philip Ridley
David Eldridge	Reginald Rose
Dario Fo	Willy Russell
Michael Frayn	Jean-Paul Sartre
John Godber	Sam Shepard
Paul Godfrey	Wole Soyinka
David Greig	Simon Stephens
John Guare	Shelagh Stephenson
Peter Handke	Peter Straughan
David Harrower	C. P. Taylor
Jonathan Harvey	Theatre Workshop
Iain Heggie	Sue Townsend
Declan Hughes	Judy Upton
Terry Johnson	Timberlake Wertenbaker
Sarah Kane	Roy Williams
Charlotte Keatley	Snoo Wilson
Barrie Keeffe	Victoria Wood

Methuen Drama Contemporary Dramatists

include

John Arden (two volumes)
Arden & D'Arcy
Peter Barnes (three volumes)
Sebastian Barry
Dermot Bolger
Edward Bond (eight volumes)
Howard Brenton
  (two volumes)
Richard Cameron
Jim Cartwright
Caryl Churchill (two volumes)
Sarah Daniels (two volumes)
Nick Darke
David Edgar (three volumes)
David Eldridge
Ben Elton
Dario Fo (two volumes)
Michael Frayn (three volumes)
David Greig
John Godber (four volumes)
Paul Godfrey
John Guare
Lee Hall (two volumes)
Peter Handke
Jonathan Harvey
  (two volumes)
Declan Hughes
Terry Johnson (three volumes)
Sarah Kane
Barrie Keeffe
Bernard-Marie Koltès
  (two volumes)
Franz Xaver Kroetz
David Lan
Bryony Lavery
Deborah Levy
Doug Lucie

David Mamet (four volumes)
Martin McDonagh
Duncan McLean
Anthony Minghella
  (two volumes)
Tom Murphy (six volumes)
Phyllis Nagy
Anthony Neilsen (two volumes)
Philip Osment
Gary Owen
Louise Page
Stewart Parker (two volumes)
Joe Penhall (two volumes)
Stephen Poliakoff
  (three volumes)
David Rabe (two volumes)
Mark Ravenhill (two volumes)
Christina Reid
Philip Ridley
Willy Russell
Eric-Emmanuel Schmitt
Ntozake Shange
Sam Shepard (two volumes)
Wole Soyinka (two volumes)
Simon Stephens (two volumes)
Shelagh Stephenson
David Storey (three volumes)
Sue Townsend
Judy Upton
Michel Vinaver
  (two volumes)
Arnold Wesker (two volumes)
Michael Wilcox
Roy Williams (three volumes)
Snoo Wilson (two volumes)
David Wood (two volumes)
Victoria Wood

Methuen Drama World Classics

include

Jean Anouilh (two volumes)
Brendan Behan
Aphra Behn
Bertolt Brecht (eight volumes)
Büchner
Bulgakov
Calderón
Čapek
Anton Chekhov
Noël Coward (eight volumes)
Feydeau (two volumes)
Eduardo De Filippo
Max Frisch
John Galsworthy
Gogol
Gorky (two volumes)
Harley Granville Barker
    (two volumes)
Victor Hugo
Henrik Ibsen (six volumes)
Jarry

Lorca (three volumes)
Marivaux
Mustapha Matura
David Mercer (two volumes)
Arthur Miller (six volumes)
Molière
Musset
Peter Nichols (two volumes)
Joe Orton
A. W. Pinero
Luigi Pirandello
Terence Rattigan
    (two volumes)
W. Somerset Maugham
    (two volumes)
August Strindberg
    (three volumes)
J. M. Synge
Ramón del Valle-Inclán
Frank Wedekind
Oscar Wilde

Methuen Drama Classical Greek Dramatists

For a complete catalogue of Methuen Drama titles
write to:

Methuen Drama
36 Soho Square
London
W1D 3QY

or you can visit our website at:

www.methuendrama.com

9 780413 733108